The Black Seminole Legacy
and
North American Politics

1693-1845

Bruce Edward Twyman

Howard University Press, Washington, DC 20001

Manufactured in the United States of America

This book is printed on acid-free paper.

10 9 8 7 6 5 4 3 2 1

Library of Congress Cataloging-in-Publication Data

Twyman, Bruce Edward, 1955–
    The Black Seminole legacy and North American politics, 1693–1845 /
    Bruce Edward Twyman.
        p.   cm.
    Includes bibliographical references and index.
    ISBN 0-88258-204-6
    1. Black Seminoies—Florida—Government relations. 2. Fugitive slaves—United States—History. 3. Afro-Americans—Florida—Relations with Indians. 4. Seminole Indians—Florida—Govemment relations. 5. Florida—History—To 1821. 6. United States—Politics and government—To 1775. 7. United States—Politics and government—1775–1783. 8. United States—Politics and government—1783–1865. 9. Seminole War, 1st, 1817–1818. 10. Seminole War, 2nd, 1835–1842. I. Title.

E185.93.F5 T87   1999
975.9′00496073—dc21

                                                                99-052746
                                                                CIP

Printed in the United States of America

Dedicated to Carrie, Edward, Tamre, Aria, Melanie, and Bruce Jr. I would like to thank many family members and friends for their help in completing this project. A few of these are Bill, Betty, Pat, Lance, Darrell, Steve, Beatrice, Luisa, and Rodney.

Contents

List of Figures

Foreword

By 1790, John Jay, George Washington, and Thomas Jefferson acknowledged that slaves fleeing to Florida was costing millions of dollars. This continuing financial loss in slave property had its origin in 1693 with the Spanish king's edict (explained below). The Black Seminoles quickly became a key foreign policy issue for George Washington's administration. The Treaty of New York in 1790 was a specific effort to recapture the Black Seminoles. If we are to view this story in its most comprehensive context, we must see it as part of Spanish-British competition in the New World. All European colonizers had slave-based economies in America; therefore, competition meant that slavery would play a major role in the struggle. The British decisively used Spanish slaves to gain a foothold in America. In their North American colonial base, the Spanish decided to use the same tactic against the British. Thus, the king of Spain issued the Edict of 1693, which promised freedom to all British slaves who could escape to Florida. The edict successfully disrupted first the British, then the U.S., regional slave industries. Finally, in 1790, Jefferson succeeded in getting the Spanish to abolish the edict.

Though members of the Washington administration acknowledged that the Edict of 1693 was the source of their problems in Florida, their method of handling this issue of runaway slaves was far different from that of their British colonial ancestors. British parliamentary records and colonial government documents show a generally unified effort to regain the fortune in slave property that had fled to Florida. However, the new U.S. Constitution provided no such luxury to the government or slave industry. The anti-slavery sentiment of the northern states would not allow the federal government to be used openly to pursue the interests of the slave industry. Except for the 13 years in which John Adams, John Quincy Adams, Martin Van Buren, and William

Henry Harrison were in office, all federal policies from 1788 to 1850 concerning the runaways in Florida were controlled by pro-slavery, if not slave-holding, presidents. Consequently, Washington inaugurated a process of using federal tax dollars to promote the interests of the slave industry in Florida, but under somewhat covert practices.

This process continued with Jefferson, Madison, Monroe, Jackson, Van Buren, Tyler, and Polk. By the 1830s, congressional abolitionists regularly attempted to disrupt the business of Congress. The House of Representatives adopted a gag rule that forbade any discussion of slavery. The Second Seminole War was raging. The pro-slavery interests successfully used the gag rule to cover up the relationship of the wars to slavery. But abolitionists in Congress discovered the cover-up. One of these men, Joshua Giddings, researched the history of the blacks in Florida, including the government's involvement. His speech to the House on the subject brought him death threats, but he was the first to reveal a cover-up going back to Washington.

In 1858, Giddings documented his finding in his book, *The Exiles of Florida:*

> Men who wielded the influence of Government for the consummation of these crimes, assiduously labored to suppress all knowledge of their guilt, to keep facts from the popular mind, to falsify the history of current events, and [to] prevent an exposure of our national turpitude. The object of this work is to meet that state of circumstances [and] to expose fraud, falsehood, treachery, and other crimes of public men, who have prostituted the powers of Government to the perpetration of murders, at the contemplation of which our humanity revolts. The author has designed to place before the public a faithful record of events appropriately falling within the purview of the proposed history; he has endeavored, as far as possible, to do justice to all concerned. Where the action of individuals is concerned, he has endeavored to make them speak for themselves, through official reports, orders, letters, or written evidences from their own hands; and he flatters himself that he has done no injustice to any person.[1]

Giddings wrote these words in the fervor of sectional conflict, but in reality it is fair to question the extent to which perspectives on the Seminoles have been shaped by previous government policy and omissions.

Note

1. Joshua Giddings, *The Exiles of Florida* (Columbus, Ohio: Follet, Foster and Co., 1858), v, vi.

Introduction

Significance of the Topic

Between the 17th and 19th centuries, a few thousand African slaves rebelled against slavery by escaping to Florida. Those slaves lived among and became identified with the Florida Native Americans known as the Seminoles. This study of the relationship between the Black Seminole rebels and the Spanish, British, and American political policies will examine political and historic events and issues not generally discussed or factored into other analyses. Since Joshua Giddings wrote *The Exiles of Florida*, scholars have documented the history of slave escapees in Florida and their armed rebellions against the slave industry. Giddings, an abolitionist congressman from Ohio, wrote *Exiles* in 1858. He follows the Seminoles from the 18th century up to their flight into Mexico in the mid-19th century. As recently as 1993, in *Freedom on the Border*, Kevin Mulroy[1] chronicled how runaway Black Seminoles used the border between the United States and Spanish Florida to remain free.

In contrast to the aforementioned studies, I specifically have sought to understand the relationship between the Black Seminoles and the political policies of Spain, Britain, and the United States. Though reports have copiously documented the existence of runaway slaves from South Carolina and Georgia among the Seminoles of Florida, the runaways have generally been depicted as third parties in the broader

1

political struggles between the British and the Spanish, between the United States and the Spanish, or between the United States and the Native Seminoles. In this type of analysis, writers have generally described the runaway slaves as an appendage to or an ally of the Spanish or the Seminoles in their struggle against Britain and United States for political empowerment and self-determination.

A closer review of these political, military, and historical conflicts would invariably reveal the nexus that exists between the runaways and the political policies of Spain, Britain, and the United States. My study begins by showing the relationship of slave rebels to the early New World politics of Spain and Britain. It is important to understand that this relationship precedes the British settlement of North America and helps establish a foundation for understanding the North American relationship.

Primarily, I will examine the relationship of slave rebels to Spanish, British, and U.S. politics between 1693 and 1845. As a result of my exploring these political relationships, the study sheds light on the rebels' relationship to (a) Spain's survival in North America between 1691 and 1821, (b) British colonial policy in the southeastern colonies until 1763, (c) the Founding Fathers' policies toward the Seminoles, (d) U.S. acquisition of Florida, (e) the Seminole Wars, (f) the presidential campaign of 1840, and (g) U.S. congressional gag rules from 1835 to 1844.

I hope my study will provide a frame of analysis for examining how the African slave traditionally responded to being placed in political bondage. Traditionally, our perspective has ranged from docile acquiescence to the limited rebellions of Gabriel Prosser, Denmark Vessey, and Nat Turner. However, a careful analysis of the Seminoles not only reveals the fact that Africans militarily rebelled against North American slavery from its beginning to 1844, but also reveals how those rebel slaves had a relationship to political policies throughout the time frame of my study.

Definitions of Concepts and Terms

Many of the words, concepts, and ideas referred to in my study have more than one meaning to researchers and readers. Therefore, I will clarify items that may predictably confuse the reader. I will also define words and phrases that may be foreign to the reader.

When the Spanish colonists arrived in the Western Hemisphere, they referred first to runaway cattle and later to Native American and African slaves as *"cimmaróns."* The word is defined as wild, as unruly, or as a runaway slave.[2] Perhaps the most common use of the term *"cimmarón"* comes in its abbreviated form, "maroon," which was originated by British and French pirates who encountered Spanish colonial society in the 16th century.[3] Another variation of *"cimmarón"* came from a renowned British seaman. During Sir Francis Drake's voyage of 1572–73, his chaplain on board referred to the rebel slaves as "symerons."[4]

By the late 17th century, both Native Americans and Africans who were slaves of the British in South Carolina escaped into Florida.[5] Those runaway slaves were technically *cimmaróns* in a Spanish colony. Between 1763 and 1783, Florida was a British colony. During this period, the combined populations of those original South Carolina *cimmaróns* and newly arriving free Native Americans, plus more African runaways from both Georgia and South Carolina, began to be identified as "Seminoles" by the British.[6] "Seminole" is an English corruption of *"cimmarón."*

For this study, "Seminoles" or "Native Seminoles" will refer to the Native Americans in Florida after 1763. "Seminoles" will also be used at times to refer collectively to both Native Americans of Florida and the runaway Africans among them. "Black Seminoles" will refer to Africans who joined the bands of "Indians."

By definition, a "rebel" is one who opposes or disobeys authority and control or who takes arms against the government or ruler of a country.[7] The enslavement of Africans by Europeans in the Western Hemisphere was a prelude to the subsequent oppression of blacks through contemporary times, from Brazil to the United States. Slaves who fled to gain their freedom and those who fought to maintain it were definitively rebels. They were the first African rebels of the Western Hemisphere and the predecessors of blacks who oppose today's authorities. Though *"cimmarón,"* "maroon," and "Seminole" accurately describe them, in most cases this study will refer to them as "rebels." In some instances for the sake of clarity, a prefix such as *"cimmarón,"* "maroon," "African," "black," or "Seminole" will be added to "rebel."

This study seeks to explain the relationship between Black Seminole rebels and North American politics. "Relationship" is defined as any connection, association, or involvement—direct or indirect—

between the rebels and politics. For this study, "politics" refers to any direct or indirect reference, comment, or acts made by politicians, administrators, or military leaders. Most of those responses are letters or governmental documents that discuss government efforts to end the rebel threat to the slave industry. Individual responses are often the puzzle pieces that reflect greater trends or emerging policies. At times, the text will discuss legislative and executive policies that have a direct relationship to the rebels. North American politics can refer to the governmental structures of colonial Spain, Britain, and the United States at the national and local levels. Native Americans are commonly referred to as "Indians." In this study, I will generally use their tribal names unless for the sake of clarity "native," "Native American," or even "Indian" would be more appropriate.

Notes

1. Kevin Mulroy, *Freedom on the Border* (Lubbock, Tex.: Texas Tech University Press, 1993).

2. For a detailed explanation of the word *"cimmarón,"* refer to Mariano Velazquez de la Cadena, *New Revised Velazquez Spanish and English Dictionary* (Chicago: Follett Publishing Co., 1974); Richard Price, ed., *Maroon Societies: Rebel Slave Communities in the Americas* (Baltimore: Johns Hopkins University Press, 1979), 1–2.

3. For a detailed explanation of the word "maroon," refer to Catherine Schwarz, ed., *Chambers Concise Dictionary* (Edinburgh: W and R Chambers Ltd., 1988); Price, *Maroon Societies*, 1–2.

4. Philip Nichols, "Sir Francis Drake Revived," in *Documents Concerning English Voyages to the Spanish Main, 1569–1580*, vol. 71, ed. Irene A. Wright (1628; reprint, Nendeln, Liechtenstein: Kraus Reprint Ltd., 1932), 259.

5. Public Record Office, "America and the West Indies, 1681–1685," *Calendar of State Papers, Colonial Series* (1898; reprint, Nendeln, Liechtenstein: Kraus Reprint Ltd., 1964), 187; Jane Landers, "African Presence in Early Spanish Colonization of the Caribbean and the Southeastern Borderlands," in *Columbian Consequences*, vol. 2, ed. David Hurst Thomas (Washington, D.C.: Smithsonian Institution Press, 1989).

6. Robert Weir, *Colonial South Carolina* (Milwood, N.Y.: Kraus Thomson Ltd., 1983), 31; Giddings, *Exiles*, 1–3; William C. Sturtevant, "Creek into Seminole," in *North American Indians in Historical Perspective*, ed. Eleanor B. Leacock and Nancy O. Lurie (New York: Random House, 1971), 92–105; James W. Covington, *The Seminoles of Florida* (Gainesville, Fla.: University Press of Florida, 1993), 3–5.

7. Use of the word "rebel" is explained in *Webster's Third New International Dictionary* (Springfield, Mass.: G. and C. Merriam Co., 1961).

Section A

Three Allies in Florida: Africans, Natives, and Spaniards

The first three chapters describe how a people known as "Seminoles" came to exist in Florida, how those people became allies of the Spanish in Florida, and how the allies helped the Spanish prevail in Florida against attacks from Britain and the United States.

Also in these chapters, I will show how Spanish policymakers crafted specific policies to help strengthen Spain's relationship with African slave rebels from South Carolina, Georgia, and Florida. The Spanish policies were crafted in the 17th and 18th centuries and were based on the Black Seminoles' presence in Florida; however, their political impact has been documented well into the 19th century.

Chapter 1

Relationships between Native and Black Seminoles

R ebel slave communities existed throughout the Western Hemisphere during the history of enslavement. In his comprehensive hemispheric study *Maroon Societies: Rebel Slave Communities in the Americas*,[1] Richard Price details the vast extent of rebellion. As we survey the phenomenon of rebellion in the Western Hemisphere under Spain, Britain, France, Portugal, Holland, and the United States, it is useful to categorize several levels of rebellion (see figure A). Too often the existence of Africans during the years of enslavement in America has been trivialized. The categories mentioned give some indication of the complexity and success of African resistance to slavery.

Level A rebellion applies to slaves who escape but pose no threat to anyone except perhaps their masters. Rebellion at this level may consist of a few individuals hiding out in the forest, mountains, and swamps, or there may be a larger number of rebels. The key characteristic at level A is that the threat, if any, to the institution of slavery and to the government is at most local. A few runaways could never threaten the government. Even a larger number of runaways at this level are easily subdued. In general, their impact is on a few plantations or is of short duration. Level A rebellion can range from single individuals who escape, to the limited rebellion of Nat Turner. Because of the relatively minimal extent of its threat, level A can be referred to as "micro-level rebellion."

Figure A – Levels of Slave Rebellions

	Central Government Control	Lack of Central Government Control	Treaty and/or Concessions to Rebels by Central Government	Alliance to Powers Hostile to Central Government	Regional Autonomy	Creation of Sovereign State
A-Micro	X					
B-Macro		X			X	
C-Macro		X	X		X	
D-Macro		X		X	X	
E-Macro						X

Level B rebels are able to prevent re-enslavement only through the use of offensive and defensive guerrilla warfare.[2] Level B rebels not only can prevent capture by the local authorities but also can resist any military overtures by the national or colonial government. At this level, communities are formed with the number of inhabitants ranging from a few dozen to thousands of members. These rebel societies are autonomous as long as they can successfully resist the government's military authority. Perhaps the best example of level B rebellion is the Brazilian slave settlement, or *quilomba*, Palmares. Palmares had approximately 15,000–20,000 inhabitants. For a century, between 1597 and 1697, those rebels successfully defeated all efforts of the Portuguese and Dutch colonial governments to destroy and re-enslave them. R. K. Kent[3] describes Palmares as a "Negro Republic," with a king who resided in a capital city. The capital contained the king's palace, ruling officials, including a police force, and 1,500 houses. In one of the smaller towns, the king's brother ruled over a village of 800 houses. This city was only for the training of soldiers.

Level C rebellion is similar to level B. Level C is distinguished by the fact that the government acknowledges its inability to conquer the rebels and concedes certain territorial and political gains. This process is formally concluded with a treaty. An example of level C rebellion occurred in Mexico. By 1608, an Angolan slave, Yanga, established a rebel community of approximately 200 inhabitants. After successfully resisting the efforts of the Spanish military for several years, Yanga was able to sign a treaty with Spain. He was made governor of San Lorenzo de los Negros in exchange for ceasing his attacks on the Spanish colonial government.[4]

Level D rebellions occurred in the context of European competition for the Western Hemisphere. Rebels fled to governments or to Native Americans who were opposed to the rebels' masters. In exchange for assurances of freedom and sometimes land or other resources, rebels fought against their former masters and helped to free other slaves. The Black Seminoles were precisely this type of rebels, as my study will reveal.

Level E rebellion was the rarest of all. It occurred only in the French colony of St. Domingo. At this level of rebellion, the slave population was so much greater than the white population—and its military force became so overwhelming—that the rebels were able to overthrow the government and replace it with their own leaders. These rebels created the Haitian republic.[5]

Levels B, C, D, and E can be referred to as "macro-level" rebellion (MLR), because in scale and scope the rebels have become an effective guerrilla force that is able to resist the efforts of the national government. Their autonomy and survival are maintained by one thing only: guerrilla warfare. The rebels' success in warfare permitted them to orchestrate their fate in the context of governments that had sought to oppress them. The Spanish, British, and U.S. political-economic systems depended heavily on African slavery during the periods included in my study. Therefore, the military success of the Seminole rebels allowed them to interdict the normal flow of government. Success in warfare yields a reciprocal political response. The political responses—to whatever degree they occur—provide the fruits for analysis. This result is underscored by the extensive writings of the noted 19th-century military strategist and political scientist Karl von Clausewitz. According to Clausewitz, "[T]he political object, as the original motive of the war, will be the standard for determining both the aim of the military force and also the amount of effort to be made." Therefore, he concludes, "[W]ar is not merely a political act but also a real political instrument, a continuation of political commerce. . . . Policy, therefore, is interwoven with the whole notion of war and must exercise a continuous action upon it."[6]

Because it existed solely as a by-product of military force, we will study MLR as a political commodity. As such, it provides the foundation and basis for seeking a reciprocal relationship to it in the politics of Spain, Britain, and the United States. The efforts of governments to suppress MLR led to war. The resulting wars were "political commerce." In this regard, the battlefields existed parallel to the legislative chamber. Policy outcome was decided by soldiers. To the extent that political strategy for the rebels was executed and devised by the same individuals, the scope and depth of any political activities can be best understood by a study of how the opposing governments responded to them.

Rebel policies or decisions regarding freedom were usually contingent on the necessities of and outcome on the battlefield. Also, rebel slaves were generally not part of an extensive chain of command. However, the soldiers that opposed them were usually employed to execute the policy of the national government. There may have been several layers of bureaucracy between the soldier and the origin of the policy. The soldier met the rebels on the battlefield. In a political context, the battlefield was transformed into a quasi legislature from which the throes of warfare could dictate the policy outcomes. However, while the policy results were not likely to reverberate far beyond the individual rebel, in the opposing governments we can observe multiple levels of bureaucratic reaction to the success or failure of policy. This bureaucratic reaction furnishes the basis for examining the political relationship between MLR and Spain, Britain, or the United States. Consequently, my study reveals the relationship between North American politics and the Seminole rebels in Florida.

Who Are the Black Seminole Rebels?

We will study the political relationship between the Black Seminole rebels and Spain, Britain, and the United States. But as this process ensues, it is important to remain cognizant of the context in which such rebels existed. As level D rebels, they participated in alliances. Therefore, it is essential to distinguish between bureaucratic reaction to the rebels and to the allies in general.

As this study reveals, various political documents draw clear distinctions between the allies and the rebels. The identity and role of African rebels in alliance with Spain, between 1693 and 1763, is not problematic. In the context of Spanish Florida, the phenomenon of MLR existed at level D. The study will show that the freedom of the rebels was challenged on numerous occasions by the British government. But the phenomenon of level D rebellion also existed from about 1790 to 1842, while the rebels were again allies of both Spain and the Seminoles until 1821, and in alliance with the Seminoles only from 1821 to 1842.

Any clear understanding of the political reaction to the Florida rebels requires a review of two issues that are germane to the alliance of Native and Black Seminoles: first, the distinction between *"cimmaróns"* and "Seminoles," and second, the Native American enslavement of Africans in the Southeast. These two issues must be explored because government records and especially scholarly research on the Seminoles too often fail to distinguish between the rebels and the natives. As a result, the role of Africans is often minimized or subverted. When this minimalization happens, political reaction to the rebels can be attributed to the Native Americans. Should this lack of distinction between natives and blacks occur often enough, the premise of my study would become moot.

Clarifying the distinction between "Seminole" and *"cimmarón,"* as well as clarifying the issue of native enslavement of Africans, will bring greater understanding of the rebels' relationship to North American politics. In the earlier Definitions of Concepts section, "Seminole" has been defined in the most accurate and comprehensive way possible. Nevertheless, there are generally two perspectives on the origin of the Seminoles (see figure B). The first perspective can be termed "mono-genesis," and the second "poly-genesis." The mono-genesis view is more popular. According to this view, the Seminoles are essentially an amalgam of the Creek Confederation, which migrated from Georgia into Florida and incorporated the few remnants of the nearly extinct Florida natives. The Seminoles are seen as originating about the time of the British occupation, though the Creek influx is believed to have continued into the 19th century. The African presence is explained as either runaway slaves permitted to settle or as Seminoles' slaves, who were bought or captured from white settlers.[7] The second and less popular perspective ascribes to a poly-genesis view. According to this view, the first Seminoles were Africans and Native Americans who fled to Florida to escape British slavery in South Carolina. From this perspective, it is asserted that the migration of Africans and Yamasees and Apalachees (both said to be branches of the Creek Confederation) began in the 1680s.[8] The second view merges the original migrants with the larger Creek migration in the mid-18th century. The mono-genesis

Figure B – Florida Immigrants Who Become Part of the Seminole People by 1763

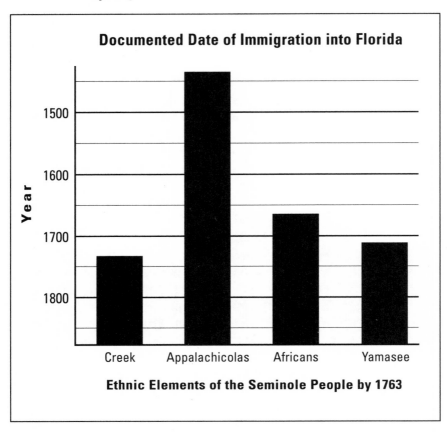

view does acknowledge that the Creeks absorbed the Native Americans who had been present in Florida long before the Creeks' arrival. However, those who accept mono-genesis are forced to ignore an existing military relationship between the non-Creek Native Americans and the Africans from British colonies, which had existed for several generations. Thus, the mono-genesis view also is mono-racial. The poly-genesis view suggests that the pre-existing alliance of earlier natives and blacks was never destroyed by Creek immigration.

Implicit in the poly-genesis view is the idea of rebel continuity from 1693 until 1842, and I have based my study on the premise of continuity. I have theorized that the continuous existence of a considerable number of autonomous rebels is the best explanation for the perplexing alliance between the Africans and the natives in Florida. That theory also best explains the concept of slavery between these two allies.

This study asserts that a state of level D macro-rebellion existed in Florida from 1693 to 1842. Therefore, rebels existed with their allies and were able to militarily defend their freedom. One clue that helps to support this assertion is the etymological linkage between the words "Seminole" and *"cimmarón."* Some scholars who hold the mono-genesis view on the origin of the Seminoles say that the word "Seminole" comes from *"cimmarón."* Then they add that "Seminole" refers not to runaway slaves but to Creek migrants in Florida who broke away from the Creek confederacy.[9] However, because the term "Seminole" was originated during the British occupation, an English word could have been used if the word was intended to refer only to Creek migrants.

As mentioned earlier, the British spelled *"cimmarón"* as "symeron" during Drake's 1572 voyage. In that case, there was no change in meaning. It is, therefore, possible that the similarly derived "Seminole" retained some of the meaning from its etymological origin. If so, that original linkage may show roots from either black or native *cimmaróns.*

Between 1693 and 1763, an alliance of Spaniards, Muscogee-speaking Yamasees and Apalachees, and African rebels existed.[10] This alliance was especially complicated by intermarriage between the African men of St. Augustine, Florida, and the native women in regional villages. Nevertheless, records indicate that the Spanish evacuated all of their black allies to Cuba when British occupation began in 1763. This move prevented their re-enslavement by the masters from whom they had fled.[11]

We have no clear record of the number of Africans who fled from South Carolina and Georgia into Florida. Even if many African rebels remained in Florida among Indians or in the swamps, it may have been impossible for them to be found or detected if they sought to evade the British. The first extensive effort to explore and chart Florida came during the Second Seminole War between 1835 and 1842. During this war, the best efforts of thousands of U.S. soldiers to find Black Seminoles and Native Seminoles proved that those rebels could easily evade capture or detection for many years.[12]

The British naturalist William Bartram[13] did extensive research in South Carolina, Georgia, and Florida between 1773 and 1776. He reported some assimilation of Spanish culture among the Seminoles in

Florida. Bartram made no reports about any Africans among them; however, though he traveled in a region of America where the slave population perhaps exceeded the white, he essentially said nothing of the slaves. Therefore, his silence about blacks among the Seminoles does not preclude their existence.

To the extent that the Seminoles mentioned by Bartram had ties to the earlier Spanish, then it is possible that some Africans from the alliance were also present. Some linkage between blacks and natives may have endured even after the Spanish departure. In addition to having formed family links, Africans had also assimilated some of the Muscogee language and culture, and old alliances between Africans and Yamasees preceded the flight into Florida.[14]

The pre-British alliance of natives and Africans forged bonds that could have assisted a merger with Creeks emigrating into Florida. Some Creek emigrants had been allies of the British and, as such, had participated in wars against the Florida allies. However, even in alliance with Britain, they could not conquer Florida. Therefore, to the extent that Africans and natives were still present after the Spanish departure, in the absence of military dominance by Creek emigrants, linguistic similarities would have helped in the assimilation of the allies and Creeks on an equal basis.

It is unlikely that all Africans who had fled into Florida were evacuated with the Spanish. In all probability only those most closely associated with Spain left. Even though Spain—and later Britain—had political rights to all of the Florida territory, for all practical purposes their administrative authority extended only to a small region around the capital. During the Second Seminole War in the 1830s, U.S. commander General Thomas Jesup informed Secretary of War Joel Poinsett that Florida was an unexplored wilderness, "the interior of which we are as ignorant as the interior of China."[15] With only a fraction of the later U.S. manpower and resources in Florida, it is unlikely that colonial Spain or Britain was any better informed about the number or location of rebel African slaves.

Even if most rebels were transported out, others continued to flee into Florida after 1763.[16] By 1771, more than half of the inhabitants in British Florida consisted of newly imported African slaves. The slave population ranged from 1,000 to 3,000 during this period. However, during the American Revolution, from 1776 to 1783, British refugees from the Carolinas and Georgia fled to Florida with their slaves. By 1783, there were up to 12,000 slaves and 9,000 whites.[17]

British colonial records indicate that the Seminoles stole slaves from British plantations. The issue of greatest concern in the short history of the Florida Colonial Assembly, 1781–84, was punishing slaves for murder and rebellion.[18] Therefore, it does seem probable that after 1763 rebels continued to exist among the natives of Florida.

In 1784, with the British loss of the Revolution, Spain regained title to Florida. Population statistics during and after the Revolutionary War are inconclusive. In *Loyalist in East Florida*, Wilbur H. Siebert reports that 6,540 blacks and 3,398 whites were evacuated by the British.[19] A Spanish census reported that 6,000 blacks and whites were evacuated. Florida Governor Patrick Tonyn reported that 4,000 refugees had passed into the U.S. interior.[20] Also, the British processed claims for hundreds of lost, stolen, or runaway slaves in Florida after the evacuation.[21]

During the British occupation, it was likely that many rebels remained in Florida and continued assisting in the rebellion of other slaves. But even if none were left from the first era of Spanish occupation, the consistency and growth of British slavery continued to yield rebels to the interior of Florida. Among the first orders of business for the new U.S. government was to stop the flow of rebels into Florida.[22]

Any interaction between rebels and natives in Florida during the years of British occupation provided the physical linkage that supports etymological ties between the words "Seminole" and *"cimmarón."* Also, this linkage fosters the continued presence of macro-level rebellion in Florida. The continuous presence of militarily autonomous rebels helps explain African slavery and the "Five Civilized Tribes." In spite of a common notion that Native Americans essentially held amicable and even benevolent or fraternal feelings toward the enslaved African in North America, some native peoples held Africans as slaves. Slavery was encouraged by the British in the southeastern colonies, and apparently those with European fathers and native mothers were the key participants.[23] Neither the British colonial government nor the United States would allow a neutral policy by natives on the subject of slavery. Even before the Washington administration, the Continental Congress had stipulations in treaties with at least 13 native peoples for the return of escaped slaves.[24]

In *American Indian Policy and American Reform*, Christine Bolt explains that in the latter days of British colonization, it was only in the Carolinas and Georgia that the black, white, and red races were numerically strong and racially and culturally interrelated. Bolt describes the white population's fear that the Africans and natives would unite to oppose the whites. Consequently, she indicates that whites convinced members of the "Five Civilized Tribes" to adopt white biases toward Africans and to assimilate European racist attitudes toward them.[25] The Cherokees, Chickasaws, Creeks, Choctaws, and Seminoles were known as the Five Civilized Tribes because they gradually attempted to assimilate the lifestyle of southern whites, primarily by rejecting "hunting and gathering" for survival and adopting in its place an economy arising from slave-based agriculture.[26]

Except for the Seminoles, the Five Civilized Tribes produced written constitutions that included slave codes. Although slavery among the tribes was perhaps milder than among whites, many instances of cruelty to Africans still occurred.[27] The institution of slavery began among the Five Civilized Tribes during colonialism and continued until the Civil War. Each tribe signed treaties and entered the Civil War on the side of the Confederacy.[28]

Although relations between Cherokees, Choctaws, Chickasaws, and Creeks and their African slaves are fairly clear and unambiguous, the situation concerning the Seminoles is just the opposite. On the one hand, slavery did exist among the Seminoles. But it has been described as a system in which the bonds between master and slave were so tenuous that slaves usually lived miles away from their Indian masters and paid only a small percentage of crops or livestock annually to their so-called owners.[29] On the other hand, U.S. congressional documents from at least 1821 to 1842 specifically stated that "Negroes govern the Seminole Indians." This documentation was submitted to Congress by Florida governors, Seminole Indian agents, U.S. army generals, and slave-holding citizens of Florida.[30]

Even though the resources indicate that both slave and free blacks lived among the Seminoles, at times all blacks were referred to as "the slaves" who "rule" the Seminoles. This type of documentation contradicts and tends to refute the idea of African slavery among the Seminoles. In *The Florida Wars*, Virginia Peters verifies that even though total proof of the precise relationship between the black and red Seminoles has not come to light, obviously it was one in which allies protected allies. Native Seminoles sought to protect their black allies from the claims of whites. Peters notes that the correspondence of military officers shows that they were unwilling or incapable of perceiving Black Seminoles with the same dignity that they accorded

Native Seminoles. She notes that one exception to the biased portrayal of Black Seminoles during the period was in the reports of Congressman Joshua Giddings.[31]

Joshua Giddings represented the state of Ohio from 1838 to 1859. As chairman of the House Committee on Claims in 1839, Giddings opposed appropriations for the Second Seminole War. He believed that the war was an effort in support of slavery. According to Giddings, U.S. policies concerning the Seminoles had all been crafted by a federal government that, since Washington and Jefferson, had been dominated by the institution of slavery. He therefore concluded that all knowledge about the Seminoles was tainted by the interests of slaveholders.[32]

If we consider Giddings's comments, it is important to understand that all presidents between 1788 and 1840 who served two terms were slaveholders. Only John Adams, John Quincy Adams, and Martin Van Buren were in office one term. As my study will show, the slave-holding presidents had the greatest influence over the federal Seminole policy. Those slave-holding presidents (Washington, Jefferson, Madison, Monroe, and Jackson) were in office for a total of 40 years as opposed to 12 years for the others. They certainly had a greater interest in and opportunity to shape the federal policy toward slavery, which included the institution of slavery among the Five Civilized Tribes, as well as the gathering and dispersal of information about the Native and Black Seminoles.

Nonetheless, it was these same federal sources, in the context of the First and Second Seminole Wars, who went to great lengths to insist that the roles of master and slave between Africans and natives had been reversed. Such contradictory statements can best be explained by the continued presence of a macro-level rebellion. Through the alliances with Spain and the Indians of Florida, rebel slaves were capable of resisting slavery from 1693 until 1842. This macro-rebellion capability apparently withstood the efforts of Native Americans in Florida. Slavery among the Cherokees, Chickasaws, Choctaws, and Creeks has been described as severe; only the Seminoles are described as benevolent masters. Between 1820 and 1837, the slave population among the Five Civilized Tribes ranged from 2 percent to 20 percent of the native total. However, only among the Seminoles is a free rebel population accounted for. The rebels were 20 percent of the total Seminole population, and the slaves were described as autonomous from the natives. Also, a steady flow of slaves is said to have run to the Seminoles.[33]

The continued presence of the macro-rebellion is the best explanation for the unique lifestyle of Africans in Florida. Any desire of immigrant Creeks to enslave Africans was most likely scrutinized by the rebels. A type of benevolent sharecropping is described between natives and Africans. But why would such a system exist only in Florida? The Native Seminoles were a branch of the Creeks, who practiced a relatively harsh form of slavery. If Native Seminoles had actually mastered the Africans, who could have compelled them to be so benevolent? It seems that a large group of armed, autonomous rebels is the best explanation. The relationship may ultimately have not been one of master and slave. The relationship between the rebels and Seminoles was both old and complex. Peters believes that Native Seminoles claimed all Africans among them as slaves as a political ploy to protect them from U.S. slaveholders. Such a theory has credence because the U.S. government certainly recognized the natives as legal political entities. Because of a greater familiarity with whites, rebel leaders often functioned as the interpreters, or intermediaries, between natives and the United States.[34] It seems they encouraged the idea of native slavery as a legal barrier to the U.S. claims on the slaves. Native claims actually provided court challenges to the claims of U.S. citizens.[35]

The rebels' position as intermediaries caused U.S. officials to point to the rebels' control over natives. In seeking to determine the true status of Africans among the Seminoles, nothing presents as great a quandary as the correspondence of American officials during the Seminole Wars. The rebels are described as the group who would determine war or peace with the United States; also they were accused of killing Native Seminoles who violated their decisions.[36]

There is a lack of precise information about the relationship between the Black and Native Seminoles. Very few sources document the beliefs of the rebels themselves. Most data concerning the Seminoles came from individuals who had some relationship to the slave industry, which sought to reclaim a fortune in lost slave property living among the natives in Florida. Joshua Giddings believed that federal resources on the subject were tainted by such a bias.

Sources that contend that the rebels were slaves of the natives must be viewed as parallel to those that project them as leaders among the Seminoles. Although it is possible that some Africans were subjected to enslavement by the Seminoles, I take the position that it was not possible for the native seminoles to physically enslave the masses of rebels in Florida. Sources describe the relations between the two as ranging from autonomous Africans giving a small annual tribute to native masters, to African control and mastery of the natives.

The original Florida alliance and the cover of the swamps provided a special setting in which rebel autonomy was possible. Within this context of freedom through the alliance, it appears that rebels sought to bolster their continuous military advantage with legal challenges to the claims of whites. During the years of Spanish occupation from 1693 to 1763, and from 1784 to 1821, the British, and later the United States, generally directed all claims for slaves to the governor in St. Augustine. Therefore, any challenge to the freedom of the rebels was subjected to a rigorous two-step process. First, Spain's right to legally free British slaves was challenged; and second, Britain and the United States occasionally invaded Florida in an effort to capture the rebels. The rebels were required only to bolster Spain militarily.

In 1821, Florida became U.S. territory. My study asserts that the rebels sought to maintain their security with a similar two-step process. Though the United States possessed Florida, the U.S. government still maintained nominal respect for the property rights of natives in Florida. Rebel leaders were fully cognizant of this fact. Indeed, they were frequently present at treaty negotiations as official interpreters for the Seminoles and were naturally capable of representing their own interests.

It seems probable that the Black Seminole leaders convinced the Native Seminole chiefs to claim many blacks in Florida as their legal slaves. This tactic would have restored a tenuous shield of legal and diplomatic protection for the Florida rebels, thereby filling the vacuum left by the departure of Spain. In all probability, the rebels compensated the chiefs with agricultural products to show their appreciation for this complex alliance, which jeopardized treaties between the Seminoles and the United States.

The British and Americans had to observe and respect the Spanish legal barrier provided by the Edict of 1693, because Spain was a great European power. Therefore, a military defense of the policy was rarely needed. But the claims of native ownership of Florida rebels were given only limited credence when challenged by Georgia and Florida slaveholders. Therefore, the rebel freedom ultimately hinged on the second step of military force and, hence, on the Seminole Wars.

Evidence suggests that at all times between 1693 and 1842, an autonomous group would have prevented enslavement as it existed among the Five Civilized Tribes. Contradictory resources tend to preclude any actual Native Seminole enslavement of Africans. However, the rebel autonomy and strength in the alliance probably allowed them to project themselves as slaves. They attempted to protect their freedom legally, hoping that military efforts would not be necessary.

British and U.S. politicians, administrators, and military leaders responded both to the alliance and to the rebels specifically in their efforts to secure slavery. Spain united with the rebels to secure its hold on Florida. The complexity of the rebel existence must, therefore, be explained in context if it is to bring clarity to the Spanish, British, and U.S. political reaction to them.

Notes

1. Price, *Maroon Societies*.

2. Schwarz, *Chambers Concise Dictionary*, 459.

3. R. K. Kent, "Palmares: An African State in Brazil," in *Maroon Societies: Rebel Slave Communities in the Americas*, ed. Richard Price (Baltimore: Johns Hopkins University Press, 1979), 171–90.

4. Price, *Maroon Societies*, 93–98.

5. For a detailed history of Haiti, see Carolyn E. Fick, *The Making of Haiti* (Knoxville: University of Tennessee Press, 1990).

6. Karl von Clausewitz, *On War*, vol. 1, trans. J. J. Graham (New York: Barnes and Noble, 1956), 11–23.

7. Gatscket, an employee of the U.S. Bureau of Ethnology, believed both Yamasees and Apalachees were branches of the Creeks. Covington, *Seminoles of Florida*, 3–15, 29–30; Sturtevant, "Creek," 92–129; Mulroy, *Border*, 1–13; Albert S. Gatscket, *A Migration Legend of the Creek Indians* (1884; reprint, New York: AMS Press, 1969), 52, 65, 66, 74.

8. Weir, *Colonial South Carolina*, 31; Giddings, Exiles, 2–4.

9. Covington, *Seminoles of Florida*, 3–5; Sturtevant, "Creek," 92–105; Mulroy, *Border*, 6–8.

10. Gatscket, *Legend*, 10, 52, 62, 74.

11. Landers, "African Presence," 315–32; Mulroy, *Border*, 9.

12. John T. Sprague, *The Origin, Progress, and Conclusion of the Florida War* (1848; reprint, Gainesville, Fla.: University Press of Florida, 1964), 114, 309–10; American State Papers, 5, *Military Affairs* (Washington, D.C.: Gales and Seaton, 1832–1861), 7:135–50.

13. William Bartram, *Travels*, (1792; reprint, Savannah, Ga.: Beehive Press, 1973), 164.

14. Jane Landers, "A Free Town in Spanish Colonial Florida," *American Historical Review* 95 (February 1990): 17; United Kingdom, *Journal of the Commissioners for Trade and Plantations, 1764–1767* (London: Her Majesty's Stationery Office, 1986), 45. On assuming administrative duties in Florida, the earl of Halifax discusses the fate of Indians left on Spanish lands.

15. Sprague, *Origin*, 200.

16. Kenneth Coleman and Milton Ready, eds., "The Original Papers of Governor John Reynolds," in *The Colonial Records of Georgia*, vol. 28, part 2 (Athens, Ga.: University of Georgia Press, 1977), 191.

17. Charles Loch Mowat, *East Florida as a British Province, 1763–1784* (Gainesville, Fla.: University Press of Florida, 1964), 64–67, 126, 137.

18. Ibid., 114, 127, 129–33.

19. Wilbur H. Siebert, *Loyalist in East Florida*, vol. 1 (Deland, Fla.: Florida State Historical Society, 1929), 208.

20. Mowat, *East Florida*, 146.

21. Siebert, *Loyalist*, vol. 2, 10, 16, 19, 409, 419.

22. John C. Fitzpatrick, ed., *Journals of the Continental Congress 1774–1789*, vol. 28 (Washington, D.C.: U.S. Government Printing Office, 1933), 118; vol. 34, 326, 430–31.

23. Christine Bolt, *American Indian Policy and American Reform* (London: Allen and Unwin, 1987), 151–53.

24. Charles Kappler, ed., *Indian Affairs, Laws, and Treaties*, vol. 2 (Washington, D.C.: U.S. Government Printing Office, 1904), 4–8, 14, 16.

25. Bolt, *American Indian*, 5.

26. Ibid., 151–56; Grant Foreman, *The Five Civilized Tribes* (Norman, Okla.: University of Oklahoma Press, 1934), 1–30; Daniel F. Littlefield, preface to *The Cherokee Freedmen: From Emancipation to American Citizenship* (Westport, Conn.: Greenwood Press, 1978), 1–11; Daniel F. Littlefield, *The Chickasaw Freedmen: A People without a Country* (Westport, Conn.: Greenwood Press, 1980), 1–15.

27. Bolt, *American Indian*, 155; Littlefield, Chickasaw, 5; Littlefield, *Cherokee*, 1–11.

28. Bolt, *American Indian*, 164; Littlefield, *Chickasaw*, 19; Littlefield, *Cherokee*, 1–11; John Ross, *The Papers of Chief John Ross, 1840–1866*, vol. 2, ed. Gary E. Moulton (Norman, Okla.: University of Oklahoma Press, 1984), 488–517.

29. Covington, *Seminoles of Florida*, 29–30; Mulroy, *Border*, 7–8.

30. *Am. St. P.*, 5, *Military Affairs*, 2:411; *Am. St. P.*, 5, *Military Affairs*, 6:68–69; *Am. St. P.*, 5, *Military Affairs*, 7:832–35; Sprague, *Origin*, 309–10.

31. Virginia B. Peters, *The Florida Wars* (Hamden, Conn.: Archon Books, 1979), 98.

32. *Biographical Directory of the United States Congress* (Washington, D.C.: U.S. Government Printing Office, 1989), 1057; Giddings, *Exiles*, 35, 50, 242–44.

33. Bolt, *American Indian*, 152–55.

34. *Am. St. P.*, 2, *Indian Affairs*, 2:441; *Am. St. P.*, 5, *Military Affairs*, 6:68–69, 454 and 7:832–34.

35. *Am. St. P.*, 5, *Military Affairs*, 6:459, 460.

36. Ibid., 68–69.

Chapter 2

Black Seminole Rebels and the New World Policies of Spain and Britain

The Seminole story begins in the context of European competition for the North American continent. Spain and Portugal were the first European nations to explore and lay claim to the New World. After Columbus's first voyage to the Western Hemisphere, Pope Alexander VI, a Spaniard, issued the famous *Inter Caetera*, in which he drew an imaginary line that in effect divided the lands of the Western Hemisphere between Spain and Portugal.[1] This act by the Catholic Church included North America as part of Spain's legal territory. During the first 30 years after Columbus's entry into the Western Hemisphere, most of Spain's attention went to the West Indies and to South and Central America. But between 1520 and 1570, Spain began to fear competition in North America. This fear encouraged Spain to begin some settlement in what is today South Carolina, Georgia, and Florida.[2]

Spanish fear was warranted by ongoing British competition in Europe. This competition extended into religion, economics, and New World colonialism. Since Columbus's discoveries, Spain had reaped great wealth from the land divisions of the Catholic Church. She was probably the richest and most powerful nation in the world. However, the wealth encouraged a decline in the traditional Spanish economic base of local agriculture and manufacturers. The decline in Spanish home industries allowed England and other European nations to expand their economies by exporting to Spain.

From its position of power, Spain sought to promote the interests of the Catholic Church. This movement led to an alignment of church and state in Spain. As the power of the church grew, it began to own an increasing share of wealth in Spain, causing free thought and trade to be stifled.[3] In contrast to this development in Spain, the English king Henry VIII broke ties with the Catholic Church and embraced Protestantism. England tended to promote free thought and trade, encouraging the development of stock pools that were prepared to support colonialism. England essentially became a haven for Protestants and the protector of this new faith.[4]

Queen Elizabeth I, the daughter of Henry VIII, ordered English pirates to attack Spanish colonies, ships, and other areas of interest.[5] The voyages of Sir John Hawkins and Sir Francis Drake, while accomplishing this goal, revealed to England how vulnerable and unprotected Spain was north of Florida.[6] In 1588, Philip II of Spain sought to crush the English base of Protestantism and New World competition. He sent the 130-ship Spanish Armada to invade England, but the British navy, aided by storms, inflicted a stunning defeat on Spain and went on to gain control of the North Atlantic. This victory cleared the way for British colonization of North America.[7]

To properly view the New World conflict between Spain and Britain, one must understand that it began in Europe and that it was religious, economic, and political. Understanding the depth of the Spanish-British competition may help to clarify the role played by the rebels in North American colonial politics.

Though the Spanish still claimed all territory between Florida and Virginia, British colonization began in that very territory in the early 17th century. In 1607, Spain unsuccessfully attempted to launch a military attack on the early British Virginia colony. Also, from 1670 to 1700, Spain and its Native American allies launched continuous raids on British settlements in South Carolina, but those attacks failed as well.[8]

Long before Spain and Britain began to compete militarily in North America, both nations found that runaway African slaves affected their quest for power in the Western Hemisphere. According to Charles and Mary Beard,[9] Queen Elizabeth I ordered British pirates, such as Sir Francis Drake and Sir John Hawkins, to attack Spanish interests in the hemisphere. In *Sir Francis Drake*, George M. Thomson informs us that the voyage of 1572–73, which established Drake as Britain's leading seaman, could not have been successful without the help of Spanish *cimmaróns*.[10]

The flow of gold and silver from the New World to Spain was essential to the execution of Spanish foreign policy. A key goal of British foreign policy was the weakening of Spain. The British realized that much of the Spanish wealth flowed from Panama and that this flow was a good target for destabilization.[11]

Philip Nichols, who served on this famous voyage as Drake's chaplain, wrote about events in "Sir Francis Drake Revived."[12] According to Nichols, Drake left Plymouth, England, in 1572 with two ships and 73 men, including his two brothers. Within a few months of his attempting to raid Panama for treasure, Drake had only one ship left. Through battle, starvation, and disease, he had lost all but 28 of his crew. Both of his brothers had died. Nichols says that Drake was saved by "symerons," whom he defined as "a Black people which about eighty years past fled from the Spaniards . . . and are since grown to a nation under two Kings of their own."[13]

Drake's mission had been crippled by his attempting to raid Panama from the sea. The Symeron rebels had told him to wait five months until the rainy season ended. They had clothed, fed, housed, and medicated Drake's remaining crew during this time, and they had hidden his ship in a shallow cove. When the rains stopped, they marched through the jungles and over mountains to intercept a Spanish mule train loaded with gold and silver. The rebels added 30 men to Drake's 18 men for this mission. As a result, Drake was able to load his ship with treasure. Perhaps equally important, the rebel leader took Drake up a tall tree on top of a mountain so that Drake could see both the Atlantic Ocean and, for the first time, the Pacific Ocean. Nichols credits the rebels with making the voyage a success.[14]

Thomson credits Drake's voyage with helping to alter the course of world history. Drake's success was a political victory for the British. However, it was also a political victory for the rebels. Nichols's report seems to indicate that the rebels existed at a macro-level of rebellion. They had established towns from which they fought Spain for many years. Their goals seem to have been to free other slaves and to defeat a common foe on the battlefield. Their success further destabilized the Spanish slave system, and, because slaves were used in the mines, the rebels' alignment with Drake interrupted the flow of wealth to Spain.

Because the Spanish were their enslavers, anyone who opposed the Spanish was an ally of the rebels. For the British, perhaps, an enemy of Spain was a friend of theirs. Britain's political goal was to gain better access to the Western Hemisphere, and Drake helped to ensure the access. Thus, to whatever extent Drake helped to strengthen Britain and weaken Spain, and thus help alter the world political equation, some credit must be given to the rebels for their role.

In Jamaica there existed a second, pre–North American example of the rebel relationship to the political rivalry between Spain and Britain. According to Irene Wright in "The Spanish Resistance to the English Occupation of Jamaica, 1655–1660," Britain invaded Jamaica with 8,000 troops in 1655 and was able to capture the whole island very quickly. Except for a handful of men, the Spaniards fled to Cuba, leaving behind bands of rebels scattered about Jamaica. The few remaining Spaniards persuaded the rebels to help them resist the British. Because the governor of Jamaica had fled, the king appointed one of the remaining Spaniards, Don Cristobal Ysassi Arnaldo as governor and ordered him to try and hold on until help arrived. About 1,000 fresh troops were sent to Ysassi from Mexico and Cuba, but most of those either deserted, were killed, or were returned by Ysassi. Ysassi informed the king that he had been given refuge by the rebels at their headquarters in the mountains, the strongest place on the island. Ysassi said that with 100 men from this location he could defeat 1,000. He said he preferred to wage guerrilla war with rebel assistance rather than use other troops.

For five years, Ysassi and the rebels waged a successful guerrilla war against British occupation forces, and they could have fought longer. However, Britain and Spain each realized that the rebels held the military balance of power in Jamaica. Spain promised freedom, supplies, and the king's gratitude for their continued assistance. The British, though, were able to provide the rebels with not only promises but also tangible supplies. Therefore, the rebel leader, "Governor" Juan Bolas, led the British to Ysassi. After Bolas's defection to the British, Ysassi immediately ceased his resistance.[15]

Within a few months of taking full possession of Jamaica, Deputy Governor Sir Charles Lyttelton proclaimed Juan Bolas to be magistrate over the free black population, with all powers except life and death over his people. Bolas was given land, and he formed his own regiment: all because of his assistance to the British in capturing Jamaica.[16]

According to Carey Robinson in *The Fighting Maroons of Jamaica*, Bolas had always been neutral toward Britain and Spain, and Ysassi's major accomplishment had been to convince Bolas not to help the British for five years. From the start of British occupation of Jamaica,

Britain's General Sedgewick complained that the rebels were the real obstacle to conquest. Sedgewick acknowledged Bolas as the leader of the rebels. He noted that in 1656 the rebels burned the British headquarters and massacred 40 soldiers. Before the war ended, both British and Spanish authorities were offering freedom to the rebels. According to Robinson, the British offered the rebels freedom and the land of their choice. Subsequently, Bolas was made a colonel and a magistrate.[17]

These examples in Panama and Jamaica clearly illustrate the impact of macro-level rebellion (MLR) on the politics of Spain and Britain. Long before the British came to Central America, the Spanish authorities in Panama were sending official correspondence to the king of Spain asking for stronger measures against the *cimmaróns*, who were a threat to slavery and production.[18] Appeals from the local to the national level are a sign that the level of rebellion was macro rather than micro.[19] To the extent that war is an extension of political commerce, the battlefield was the political arena in which those conflicting policies were settled. The fact that the rebels were successful in battle meant that their goals prevailed.

When Queen Elizabeth I sent Drake to challenge the Spanish monopoly in the New World, government policy entered the political arena of the battlefield. The British desire to weaken Spain while strengthening themselves was in harmony with the ongoing policy of the Panama rebels. Britain had no conflict with the rebels. Spain simply wanted to defend its interests against both. In battle, these allies prevailed against Spanish interests. Drake gained fortune, fame, and knighthood. The queen succeeded in striking a blow at Spain, and the rebels perhaps weakened their old foes and enjoyed continued success against them.

Regarding Jamaica, the British desire to gain a rich West Indian island was part of its political strategy. Not many Spaniards or slaves were on the island, and it seems that the maroon population was minimal. But as Britain continued to press its New World policy, profound changes occurred. Britain sent 8,000 troops on 38 ships to Jamaica in an effort to gain a solid foothold in the heart of the New World. In the wake of the British invasion, the slaves escaped to the hills and forests. The invasion and defeat of the Spaniards established the freedom and autonomy of the rebels. When Ysassi sought the rebels' military assistance and promised concessions, their participation on the battlefield and in the political arena was ensured. British counteroffers to the rebels established them as decisive political players in the Spanish-British political conflict.

In the Panamanian and Jamaican examples, rebels seemed to have held the balance of power that ensured the successful execution of British political policies. The Spanish saw that their New World policies were unsuccessful. In both Panama and Jamaica, runaway slaves helped to ensure the defeat of their objectives. However, perhaps Spain did learn the value of forming political and military alliances with rebels. Strategic negotiations between Ysassi and Juan Bolos allowed Spain to remain in Jamaica for five years.

To the extent that the battlefield is a political arena for settling policy objectives, Jamaica and Panama serve as examples that demonstrate how the rebels achieved political empowerment. These cases can be seen as the beginning of a pattern in which MLR would continue to affect Spanish, British, and U.S. politics. There was no rebel political continuity from Panama and Jamaica to North America. However, the quest for the natural human right of freedom stimulated similar responses among other slaves. The slave's willingness to rebel to achieve freedom was a constant. In North America, the British switched roles with the Spanish and became the hated slaveholders.

The Spanish, perhaps learning lessons from the conflicts in Panama and Jamaica, took steps to ensure the allegiance of rebel slaves. In executing his defense of Jamaica, Ysassi informed the king of Spain that the British would soon threaten his colony in Florida. It is conceivable that the king heeded Ysassi's warning about Florida and learned some strategic lessons about alliances with rebels. A clue is that within 33 years of Spain's alliance with Jamaican rebels, the king of Spain established a similar alliance with rebels who had escaped from British colonies into Florida. In Jamaica, the rebel-Spanish alliance helped maintain a Spanish presence for five years after an apparent English conquest. However, in Florida for nearly 117 years, rebel slaves helped defend Spain in conflicts with Britain and the United States.

Notes

1. J. H. Parry and P. M. Sherlock, *A Short History of the West Indies*, 2d ed. (London: Macmillan Co., 1963), 6.

2. Herbert Ingram Priestley, *A History of American Life* (New York: Macmillan Co., 1929), 15–21.

3. Lyon Gardiner Tyler, *England in America, 1580–1652*, vol. 4 of *The American Nation: A History* (New York: Harper Brothers, 1904), 3–4.

4. Thomas A. Bailey, *The American Pageant: A History of the Republic* (Boston: D. C. Heath and Co., 1966), 11.

5. Charles and Mary Beard, *The Beards' New Basic History of the United States*, rev. William Beard (Garden City, N.Y.: Doubleday and Co., 1968), 20.

6. Tyler, *American Nation*, 7.

7. Bailey, *American Pageant*, 11.

8. George Malcolm Thomson, *Sir Francis Drake* (New York: William Morrow and Co., 1972), 94.

9. Charles and Mary Beard, *The Beards' Basic History of the United States* (New York: Doubleday, Doran and Co., 1944), 4.

10. Thomson, *Sir Francis Drake*, 94.

11. Ibid., 64.

12. Nichols, "Sir Francis Drake Revived," 254–323.

13. Ibid., 257.

14. Ibid., 310.

15. Irene A. Wright, "The Spanish Resistance to the English Occupation of Jamaica, 1655–1660," in *Transactions of the Royal Historical Society*, Series 4, vol. 13 (London: Butler and Tanner Ltd., 1930), 119–44.

16. Public Record Office, *Cal. S. P., Colonial Series, 1574–1660*, vol. 5, ed., W. Noel Sainsbury (1860; reprint, Vaduz, Liechtenstein: Kraus Reprint Ltd., 1964), 122.

17. Carey Robinson, *The Fighting Maroons of Jamaica* (Great Britain: William Collins and Sangster, 1869), 18–27.

18. Nichols, "Sir Francis Drake Revived," 9–10.

19. Robinson, *Fighting Maroons*, 1–18.

Chapter 3

The Spanish and the Rebels in Florida, 1693–1821

Twenty-one years after Columbus sailed into the West Indies, Ponce de Leon claimed Florida for Spain. By 1565, Spain had founded St. Augustine. However, long before Spain began to settle these regions, the Papal Bull of 1492 had granted all of North America, parts of South and Central America, and all of the West Indies to the Spanish. The British laid a competing claim to North America as early as 1497, after the voyages of John and Sebastian Cabot to Newfoundland.[1] The voyages of Sir John Hawkins in the 1560s revealed how militarily vulnerable Spain was throughout North America. Shortly after Hawkins, Sir Humphrey Gilbert and Sir Walter Raleigh set sail for North America to exploit the Spanish weakness. However, they were intercepted by the Spanish fleet and almost destroyed. Raleigh and Gilbert were only part of a wave of British pirates sent to attack the interests of Spain and Catholicism. Drake's triumphant voyage in 1572–73 was a devastating blow to Spain and helped to convince the Spanish king, Philip II, that drastic measures were necessary to safeguard New World territories and Catholicism. In 1588, Philip sent a 130-ship armada to invade England; however, Spain's defeat cleared the way for Britain's access to North America.[2]

The British-Spanish competition continued in North America. In 1607, Spain launched military raids on the new British colony in Jamestown, Virginia. Spain still claimed this part of North America but was unable to evict the British. By 1670, British colonization of the

Carolinas began. Not only were these new settlements in a region claimed by Spain but also they were very close to the Spanish base in Florida. With the help of Apalachee allies in Florida, Spain began to launch continuous raids on the Carolina region in an effort to destroy the British settlements.[3] Most of the military strength of Spain was centered in the West Indies and Mexico, but Florida was vital to the protection of shipping routes. Therefore, Spain saw the natives in Florida as vital allies against British encroachment. As early as 1602, Spain realized that Florida might never attract a significant population of Europeans. In spite of this realization, the Spanish fortified St. Augustine, and the Catholic Church began to convert the natives. At least three dozen missions had been constructed in Florida by 1675. Apalachees and other natives lived near the missions.[4]

Except for a brief period of British occupation, between 1763 and 1783, Florida would remain a Spanish colony until 1821. Spain maintained its presence in Florida by military strength, and, to a great extent, its armed forces depended on rebel slaves and Native Americans.[5]

This chapter will focus on the political relationship between rebels from colonial South Carolina and Georgia and those in Spanish Florida between 1693 and 1819. Because the battlefield is an extension of the political arena, by analyzing Spain's alliance with the rebels and the subsequent response to their battlefield success, we can observe some corresponding policy reactions by the Spanish colonial government.

The British policy of colonization in North America was in conflict with Spain's previous claims to the territory. As in Panama and Jamaica, the primary goal of African slaves was to obtain freedom and attack the institution of slavery. Because macro-rebellion is always a phenomenon that opposes its enslaver, runaway slaves found a natural ally in Spanish Florida.

The rebel alliance with the Spanish forced both Britain and later the United States to undergo a two-step process to threaten the rebels' freedom. Because of Spain's great-power status, rebel freedom first had to undergo a legal and diplomatic challenge. Once it was clear that this approach had failed, a military challenge became the final resort. The military challenges were the ultimate test both to macro-rebellion and to the survival of the Spanish in Florida.

The king of Spain formally recognized the utility of the Black runaways in his Edict of 1693, which freed more slaves and encouraged them to come to St. Augustine. Then, the rebels were incorporated into the Spanish military, which raided Carolina. The most formal acknowledgment of the crucial role of the Black Seminoles came in 1738 when they were established in a military garrison that guarded the entrance to the Spanish capital in Florida, St. Augustine.[6]

The utility of the Black Seminoles in Spain's maintenance of Florida is most clearly demonstrated in two major wars. In 1740, the king of England declared war on the Spanish in St. Augustine. In the war, blacks of the garrison, led by Carolina runaways, played a decisive role in defeating the British. Finally, by 1812, the U.S. Congress secretly authorized James Madison to invade and seize Florida. The Black Seminoles led a fierce counterattack, which ultimately forced Congress to withdraw troops. Also, the Washington Treaty of 1819 ceded Florida to the United States. This treaty strongly implies that the ceding of Florida to the United States was the price Spain had to pay for its long alliance with the rebels who represented millions of dollars in U.S. slave property.

The Spanish-Seminole alliance resulted in political success for Spain and for the Seminoles. In this context, blacks thrived for 126 years as level D rebels. The Seminole-Spanish alliance began as Spain sought to enforce its policy of keeping the British out of the region south of Virginia. When the British established colonies in Virginia and the Carolinas, the Spanish were determined to attack them. Opinion is divided over who first used native allies to supplement their defenses, but by the late 17th century both nations were engaged in the practice. The British attack on and enslavement of Spain's ally, the Apalachees, may have been a calculated military move that would have strengthened their ability to execute their political objectives. Although African slavery existed in Florida, as an institution its scale and impact were negligible in comparison to the slavery of the British, who developed slavery as a vital institution throughout their North American colonies. Perhaps it was only logical for Britain to weaken Spain by attacking the Apalachees and for Spain to seek to destabilize Britain by allying with its slaves. Within the last quarter of the 17th century, both policies were under way, which helped ensure the genesis of the Seminoles and their role as allies of Spain.[7]

By 1674, Dr. John Woodward signed a treaty with the natives in Carolina, thereby laying an economic foundation for the colony. The Westoes agreed to capture the Apalachee allies of Spain and to sell them as slaves to the British Carolinians. The British sold most of them to the West Indies. This policy would help to secure the frontier between Carolina and Florida by eliminating Spain's chief military ally.[8]

But the new British policy led to problems between the colonists and the proprietors in London. One early Carolinian, John Oldmixon, said that between 1682 and 1684 the proprietors forbade the enslavement of natives and that Governor Joseph Moreton and Surveyor General Maurice Matthews were removed from office for participating in the trade. The new governor, James Moore, sought to gain a monopoly over the slave trade of natives as he sought to dominate the colonial assembly, even to the extent of allowing Africans to vote. An investigation into Moore's activities was launched. He initiated a slave-catching expedition into Florida in 1702 to capture natives under the guise of combating the Spanish enemy. On this expedition, Moore was accompanied by 600 whites and 600 Yamasees, and more than 1,000 Apalachees were enslaved.[9]

James Covington believed that Moore invaded Florida with 50 whites and 1,000 Creeks. He says Moore's slave raid captured 1,300 Apalachee men, women, and children and then killed off the last independent members. The Apalachees of Florida seem to have been the key target of trading natives as slaves. Although the trade began with Dr. Woodward, by the time of Governor Moore's expedition, the supply of Apalachees was nearly exhausted.[10]

The slave trade of natives in Carolina was generally rooted in the strategic goal of disposing of the Spanish ally. Native slavery had not proved to be a stable foundation of colonization in the New World. However, the African slave industry was the economic foundation of the hemisphere. There was no reason to believe that African slaves would not replace natives as slaves in Carolina. Although thousands of natives were in the Southeast, the British regional policy tended to distinguish between the enslavement of the masses and of those who were Spanish allies.

From the beginning, Woodward notified a London proprietor, the earl of Shaftesbury, that local Westoes were hunting slaves for the British in 1674.[11] By 1680, the proprietors notified the Carolina governor, in the instructions for founding the city of Charleston, that local natives within a 200-mile radius could not be enslaved or sold out of Carolina.[12] The proprietors indicated that some colonists had been causing problems by capturing natives. It seems that many members of the regional tribes had been captured in the slave trade. The Creeks sold captured Choctaws in Charleston. The Yamasees played a major role in the Carolina slave trade involving natives. The Yamasees helped to facilitate the capture of the Apalachees, and, in order to work in concert with the British, they positioned themselves at strategic sites between St. Augustine and Carolina.[13]

The phenomenon of rebellion was a major concern for Carolina. As early as 1683, Governor Moreton assembled the legislature to discuss ways to end trading natives as slaves and to prohibit African slaves from escaping.[14] In 1689, Carolina Governor Seth Sothell received a letter from the London proprietors who advised him to "take care to prevent servants and Negroes running away to the Spanish at St. Augustine."[15] Though the Carolina political leaders do not specify the tribal ethnicity of the natives, it seems likely that those from Florida would seek to return home. Perhaps slaves from other regions would run back to their own people and to familiar surroundings. But in this case, Florida was their primary destination and African slaves accompanied them.

The establishment of colonies along the Atlantic coast from Massachusetts to the Carolinas was the fulfillment of British colonial policies. The thousands of colonists and slaves yielded prosperity and were proof of this fulfillment. In southern Carolina, a leading source of wealth until 1794 was the trade of native slaves. However, escaped African and native slaves were beginning to destabilize the colony. This destabilization proved to be bad for Britain's policy goals, yet it was very good for the runaway slaves. The natural goal, desire, or policy of slaves is to seek freedom. To the extent that Apalachees, Africans, and any other slaves escaped into Florida, they were successful in executing their policy goals, and by definition they were *cimmaróns*.

As the enemies of their British masters, the escaped slaves were naturally favored by the Spanish. Spain claimed all the land up to Virginia and perhaps feared that the British would soon get Florida unless something were done. Governor Ysassi of Jamaica had warned the king of Spain 30 years earlier that Britain would attempt to take Florida.[16] Spain launched preemptive strikes against British settlements in Virginia. In southern Carolina, Spain launched small, limited invasions in an effort to stunt the growth of the British. The surveyor-general of Charleston, Edward Randolph, reported to the London Board of Trade that in 1686 a Spanish force of 100, including blacks and Indians, raided the plantation of Governor Moreton and took 13 slaves. The invaders told the British that the Carolinas were Spanish property and that the king of Spain had ordered them not to return any slaves to the British. The invaders informed the British that the city of Charleston was really called St. Jorge. After that invasion, the new governor, James

Colleton, sought to negotiate with Spain for the return of the African slaves who had fled with the St. Augustine forces and for other Carolina slaves who daily escaped to Florida.[17] The Carolina political authorities were extremely concerned about black slaves in particular escaping to Florida. Though the trading of native slaves was the region's most valuable industry in the late 17th century, the documents reflect more concern with the maintenance of African slavery.

As the Spanish forces were invading the Charleston region, the Spanish governor at St. Augustine, Don Diego de Quiroga, informed the king of Spain that many runaway slaves from Charleston were arriving in the city. Quiroga said the slaves had informed him that they were fleeing slavery because they wanted to become Catholics. The governor said the British were pressuring St. Augustine for the release of the slaves. He asked the king what should be done with them.[18]

Even though the rebels gave the excuse of running away to become Catholic, it seems that they may have been using religion to cater to the ongoing political and military struggle between Spain and Britain. Because of the delicate military and political balance between the European colonial nations, Spain no doubt found the excuse of religion to be the most convenient one available. It is not clear whether the idea originated with the runaways or with the Spanish. But perhaps Spanish political officials were more cognizant of the political nuances inherent in European diplomatic circles than were the recently liberated slaves.[19] It seems most likely that Spain needed military allies and sought to weaken its British enemy, but by 1693, the Spanish king, Charles II, gave his answer to Governor Quiroga:

> To the Governor and Captain-general of the city of St. Augustine. . . . It has been notified in different letters, dated 1688, 1689 and 1690, that eight black males and two black females who had run away from the city of San Jorge, arrived to that presidio asking for the holy water of baptism, which they received after being instructed in Christian doctrine. Later on, the chief sergeant of San Jorge visited the city with intention to claim the runaways, but it was not proper to do so, because they had already become Christians. . . . As a prize for having adopted the Catholic doctrine and become Catholicized, as soon as you get this letter, set them all free and give them anything they need, and favor them as much as possible. I hope them to be an example, together with my generosity of what others should do. I want to be notified of the following of my instructions as soon as possible.

> Dated in Madrid, November 7th, 1693, I, the King[20]

This order from Charles II ultimately became the foundation of Spain's military and political policy in North America. Charles II became king of Spain in 1665, only 5 years after the rebels of Jamaica had been so crucial in the balance of power between Spain and Britain, and 120 years after Sir Francis Drake was supported by the rebels in Panama.

The king, who waited 5 years to answer, had the chance to assess the rebels' potential military and political significance. He had received his first letter from the governor in 1688. Before his order of 1693, Carolina citizens made numerous complaints. Governor Quiroga had promised those Carolina officials that the king would compensate them for the slaves, but not return them. However, the governor did not fulfill his promise, which prompted the St. Augustine notary to inform the king that the governor was jeopardizing the peace with Britain and threatening Florida's security. The king was informed that the British preferred the return of their slaves. Presumably, Charles II knew, therefore, that a policy of freeing the British slaves could be just as militarily significant in Florida as it had been in Jamaica.

The king implied that he wanted to encourage other Carolina slaves to come to Florida to partake of his generosity and Catholicism. In a letter regarding the manner in which Governor Quiroga handled the delicate negotiations with the British, the Spanish attorney general in Madrid reprimanded the governor: "The attorney estimates that the Governor did break his promise and did not do right, . . . especially when religion was the excuse given so as not to turn in the Negroes."[21]

It seems probable that the stated goal of catholicizing the runaways was only a diplomatic vehicle for Spain's effort to strengthen its security. Perhaps Catholicism played some part in the king's political policy goals, but no better excuse seems to have existed. The role of the Jamaican rebels may have been fresh in the minds of both nations. Spain could not bluntly say that the Spanish were undermanned in Florida and that the 1693 edict could serve the dual purpose of weakening Britain and strengthening Spain.

In spite of the Spanish excuse of religion, the British seemed to realize the military implication of the new Spanish policy. In 1698, Surveyor General Randolph informed the board of trade in London that the new order prohibited the return of runaway slaves.[22] Also, Spanish Governor Laureanode Torres y Ayala yielded to British demands and returned six black slaves and one native slave in 1697.[23]

The governor disobeyed the order of his king. In the wake of the 1693 order, the actions of both nations seemed to acknowledge that its impact would transcend the sphere of religion. The Florida governor yielded on policy to avoid conflict, and the Carolinians apparently were prepared for conflict pursuant to British policy. Ultimately, the king of Spain's Edict of 1693 established a political-military policy that drew rebels from the Southeast to freedom and that established them as a key element in Florida's defense. Though the king and the governor at St. Augustine spoke of spiritual justification, it seems obvious that neither side had any illusions about the reality of the edict.

Between 1714 and 1716, the Yamasee War took place. This war demonstrated the utility of a united black and native military force as Spanish allies. The war perhaps cemented a bond between the Africans and natives that would last until at least the 1840s. The Spanish had previously supported guerrilla forces in hit-and-run attacks on Carolina. Some Carolina runaways participated in the guerrilla attacks. But the Yamasee War was a coordinated effort to destroy the British presence in the Southeast. The Apalachees had been Britain's primary target in its Indian trade. They and the African slaves were escaping to Florida. The Yamasees and Creeks had been assisting the British in capturing slaves and were paid guns and other goods in exchange for them. The Yamasees developed a habit of going into debt with British traders. On one such occasion the British traders seized Yamasees as slaves to repay the debt. This act by the traders began the Yamasee War. Yamasees, Creeks, and Apalachees attacked the colony of South Carolina.[24]

In addition to the united stand by the natives, African slaves entered the war. According to Jane Landers:

> Blacks outnumbered Whites in the colony.... When many slaves joined the Yamasee Indian War against the British, they almost succeeded in exterminating the badly outnumbered Whites. Indians loyal to the British helped to defeat the Yamasee, who with their black allies headed for St. Augustine. Although the Carolina Assembly passed harsh legislation designed to prevent further insurrections and control the slaves, these actions and subsequent negotiations with St. Augustine failed to deter the escapes or effect the reciprocal return of slaves. British planters claimed that the Spanish policy, by drawing away their slaves, would ruin their plantation economy.[25]

According to Landers, Yamasee Chief Jorge, who led the attack on the British, said that he made alliances with African slaves before the Yamasee War.[26] There was a constant flow of Africans into St. Augustine even before the Yamasee War, and both the British and the

Spanish saw the impact of the policy. African and native slaves who fled Carolina played key roles in this attack. For the Spanish, it seemed to demonstrate the successful execution of political goals. Spain claimed the territory at least up to Virginia. Even if it was unrealistic to believe that Britain could be removed from the land, past actions demonstrated the usefulness of harassing the British to deter expansion. The Yamasee War was perhaps one of the most deadly attacks on colonial America. Though technically the British won the war, Spain successfully used it to achieve a political goal. The war also demonstrated positive aspects of the 1693 edict, which probably enhanced Spain's general goals for the region.

As a direct result of the war, Yamasees and Apalachees nearly succeeded in ending the trade of native slaves. This political goal probably could not have been successfully negotiated. Black slaves had been fleeing to Florida with Apalachees, which resulted in the 1693 edict. Both native and black slaves can be defined as *"cimmaróns."* But perhaps the genesis of what would become the Seminole people can be detected during the war in the alliances of the Yamasees and the South Carolina slaves.

Though African slavery would continue in the Carolinas, the edict provided a convenient escape. Through the edict and the Yamasee War, a durable Spanish, native, and black military alliance was forged that bolstered Spain's position in North America. At the same time, Black Seminoles and Native Seminoles became aware of their potential in the British-Spanish conflict. In the Yamasee War, both groups opposed slavery but the primary assault was on native slavery. However, the military bond that was established between natives and blacks would hold in its resistance to African slavery for almost 150 years.

The South Carolina government directed most of its wrath at the St. Augustine government instead of at the Yamasees. The South Carolinians blamed Spain for starting the war, and they were critical of the impact of the 1693 edict upon their slave industry. In a 1715 letter to Lord Charles Townsend, acting secretary of state of the Southern Province, the colonial governor of South Carolina, Charles Cravin, said that the Yamasees were primarily supported by St. Augustine. Also, he noted that one year before the war, the Yamasees had warned the traders of their intent.[27] In 1716, two agents for the Commons House, Joseph Boone and Richard Beresford, wrote to the London Board of Trade and Plantations listing numerous grievances against St. Augustine. One major complaint was the Spanish support of the Yamasee War. They also informed London that the Yamasees and others were attacking plantations and preventing their resettlement, and stealing African slaves whom they refused to return. Boone begged London to declare war on St. Augustine, and he said that many assembly agents had gone to St. Augustine to negotiate with the governor for the slaves but that they had had no success. Boone stated that the Spaniards were repaying South Carolina for capturing their natives.[28]

Between the Yamasee War and 1740, the general political objective of the British in the Southeast was to build successful colonies. Within this political context, St. Augustine and its allies were the primary threat. The legislative records are full of complaints against Spain's policy of providing freedom for South Carolina slaves. Special desertion committees were formed in the assembly to find solutions to the problem of runaway black slaves. Assemblymen notified the London proprietors that the survival of the British colonies required the destruction of St. Augustine. The desertion committee sent a petition to the king of England requesting a declaration of war; it reminded him that the king of Spain's edict had been posted throughout South Carolina and that this violated the treaty between Spain and Britain.[29]

Britain wanted to see the plantation economy of South Carolina thrive. Spain sought to undermine the growth of the colony. The Spanish policy drew many slaves into Florida. In spite of the edict drawing slaves and stating the policy of providing freedom, initially the slaves' position in St. Augustine was ambiguous. In 1725, the Florida governor, Antonio de Benavides, informed the king of Spain that because of the 1693 edict, blacks and Apalachees were still arriving.[30] By 1738, a group of runaway Carolina slaves had to petition the king for clarification of the 1693 edict because they had been either re-enslaved on arriving in St. Augustine or were made to serve indentures. In 1738, Governor Manuel de Montiano informed the king that, in violation of orders, some of the runaway slaves had been sold to local citizens of St. Augustine. Montiano stated that he had received a 1733 order that clarified the order of 1693. In this new order, the king said that under no conditions should any money be paid to the British, nor should any more British slaves be re-enslaved.[31]

One of the Carolina runaways who had petitioned the king of Spain was Francisco Menendez, a Mandingo.[32] Menendez was an ally of Yamasee Chief Jorge. Both had fought against South Carolina and had fled together into Florida. Menendez had been re-enslaved through trickery, but his condition was more indentured than enslaved. He was the leader of a black militia in St. Augustine. In his position, Menendez had helped defeat the British in a 1728 attack and had initiated the petition "The Runaway Negroes from English Plantations to the Crown." In 1738, Governor Montiano established the free Carolina blacks on a site that was 2–3 miles north of St. Augustine and was situated on Mose Creek. Mose was a presidio or fort that housed up to 200 people. The governor designated Menendez as the ruler of Mose.[33]

The new Edict of 1733 clarified the status of all British slaves arriving in Florida. However, even the most illustrious rebel, Menendez, could petition the king. It seems that this special status held by the rebel slaves was based on their military value. After being set up in Mose, the rebels had some territorial integrity. Their survival was facilitated by the Spanish, yet the Spanish prevailed against the British with the help of the Mose rebels. Therefore, the freedom of those rebels was ensured only through military force.

In 1727, the Tribunal of the Indies informed Madrid that the British considered the 1693 edict an attraction to their slaves; they felt that it was designed to help Spain and hurt them and that warfare was imminent.[34] By 1739, in a letter to the king, Montiano first informed the king that Mose was established because the Edicts of 1693 and 1733 said to favor them as Catholics, but in the same letter Montiano said St. Augustine would soon fight a war with Britain. He said the runaways were needed in the army, and the fort would attract more of them. Also, he informed the king that 23 more had just arrived.[35]

In 1740, the British launched their heaviest assualt on the Spanish government in St. Augustine. In 1739, the South Carolina legislature had received a declaration of war from the king of England. The legislature provided 2,000 native troops, 2,200 white men, black laborers with enough white men to guard them, and seven warships. This force was led by Georgia founder Colonel James Oglethorpe.[36] Oglethorpe declared, "[A]s his majesty had ordered... [s]pare no personal labor nor danger towards freeing Carolina of a place from whence their Negroes were encouraged to massacre their masters and were openly harbored after such attempts."[37]

Oglethorpe warned the government of South Carolina that troops had to move quickly and that the fleet had to blockade St. Augustine so that Spanish reinforcements could not come from Havana. He completely surrounded St. Augustine. When he arrived at Fort Mose (the British called it "Moosa"), it was deserted. Nearly 200 British troops were stationed there. Day and night, from land and sea, the British cannons bombarded St. Augustine. The only way to assault St. Augustine on the ground was from Fort Mose, and, likewise, any Spanish defensive assault had to encounter Mose. At 4 A.M., 15 June 1740, 300 rebels and natives captured Fort Mose; 80 British were killed and 25 were taken prisoner. Most of the British casualties occurred during this encounter. Oglethorpe's scattered forces were afraid of being picked off by the rebels. Within 3 weeks, the British forces evacuated. According to a Spanish prisoner, the white Spanish forces stayed within the St. Augustine fort during the war.[38]

Menendez and the militia kept track of the British forces as they began their invasion of Florida, and he led the attack that devastated the British. Governor Montiano asked the king to give Menendez a special commendation for his leadership. Montiano depended on the Mose militia to a greater extent than did any other Florida governor. Oglethorpe would initiate several more attacks on St. Augustine, but none were on the scale of the 1740 war. Menendez exploited the Spanish-British rivalry to obtain concessions from Montiano. The white Spanish military forces were few in Florida. The Mose militia were used in land and sea campaigns against South Carolina and Georgia. Montiano refused to launch corsair naval raids without the Mose forces. British attacks in the 1740s destroyed Mose, and the militia was evacuated to St. Augustine. However, by 1752, Mose was rebuilt and reoccupied.[39]

It seems that Spanish Florida overwhelmingly depended on auxiliary forces for its survival, and so, as the British Empire in North America grew, Spanish authorities made certain that Mose was prepared. In a letter from Don Alonso Fernandez to Father Don Julian de Arriaga in 1756, the following comments were made:

> The village of Mose, close to this city, is habitated by the fugitive Negroes from the English colonies who arrived here to be baptized and were freed . . . and have organized a company with a Captain, Lieutenant, and Sargeant. The city works now as an advanced post. The Negroes have their lands to cultivate and support themselves without costing you any money. I sent an engineer out to plan and construct defenses and canyons. I also assigned a Franciscan Friar to teach them religion. I asked the Viceroy of Mexico to give him the same salary other missionaries make among Indians.[40]

These comments indicate the extent to which the rebels were vital to Florida. Though the British had managed to destroy Mose, it was rebuilt and fortified. More attacks were expected. Mose was the first line of defense. If Mose fell, eventually St. Augustine could too. Mose's significance is further underscored in a 1759 letter to the governor of Florida from Madrid: "One of your requests from August 20, 1758, was to assign financial aid to the Negroes of Mose, for several reasons. The King wants you to assign whatever you consider necessary to help them . . . make arrangements to distribute aid between the Negroes of the Village of Mose."[41]

The position of the Spanish authorities toward the British runaways by 1759 contrasts sharply with the hesitance and ambiguity displayed between the 1680s and the 1740 British invasion. Though Spain never dropped its insistence on the use of the religious "excuse," as early as the 1750s the records indicate that Mose was militarily essential as an advanced post. Ironically, though the Spanish successfully defended Florida from military conquest, by 1763, the Treaty of Paris which ended the Seven Years' War and the French and Indian War, would grant Florida to the British.[42] However, in the 1783 Treaty of Paris, which ended the American Revolution, the British came to terms with the United States and many other nations in a world war. Spain then reoccupied Florida.[43]

During the British occupation, the Seminole population was no longer centralized near St. Augustine. Their settlements were scattered from St. Augustine to Pensacola.

After the American Revolution, the return of Florida to the Spanish meant the continuation of the king's Edicts of 1693 and 1733. John Jay, as secretary of state for the Continental Congress, informed Thomas Jefferson of the devastation the Seminoles had brought on the state of Georgia. Jefferson was told that the edicts must be repealed and that Spain should be punished.[44] Though the edicts were in fact repealed, the Spanish made no efforts to return slaves, as they had also promised.

As in the previous century, the Florida problem became so intense that in 1811 President James Madison called a secret session of both houses of Congress. After 31 votes were taken, a resolution was passed that authorized President Madison to use military force to seize Florida.[45] This venture was known as the Patriots War because Madison attempted to plant patriotic Americans in Florida and then overthrow the St. Augustine government.[46] But the same pattern of events occurred as in 1740. By 1811, Spain was even weaker in Florida than it had been in the 18th century. As the United States laid siege to St. Augustine, the Spaniards held fast in the fort. Florida's Governor

Juan Estrada sent word to the various Seminole camps. The Seminoles launched guerrilla attacks on the U.S. forces and eventually forced them to retreat back to Georgia. The settlements of the patriots were also driven out. As was the case in 1740, the Spaniards were able to keep Florida without leaving the well-constructed fort of St. Augustine.[47]

According to Covington, former Georgia Governor Mathews unsuccessfully sought the Seminoles' help in seizing Florida.[48] Though the efforts initiated by Madison ended in 1813, the state of Georgia continued unsuccessfully to try to seize Florida. In *The Plot to Steal Florida*, Joshua B. Smith comments on the historical and symbolic importance of the U.S.-supported forces pausing at the ruins of old Fort Mose. Smith believed that this act indicated that the struggle had become a racial conflict. He notes the destruction and rebuilding of Fort Mose during the Spanish colonial era. Also, he says that Florida Governor Estrada attempted to reconstruct Mose in 1811 when he learned of the U.S. plans to invade, but the Americans arrived too soon.[49]

The Patriots War demonstrated to the U.S. government that Spain was essentially powerless in Florida. In spite of Spain's prevailing over U.S. forces, key American government officials recognized that the Seminoles were the military might behind the victory. The commander of U.S. forces notified Secretary of State James Monroe that the principal military strength in Florida consisted of rebel slaves who bolstered the Spanish.[50]

U.S. military initiatives subsequent to the Patriots War ignored the Spanish presence except to scorn its weakness. Indeed, members of Congress and President James Monroe observed that Spain's political authority was confined to the city of St. Augustine. U.S. officials declared the Seminoles to be a sovereign force unto themselves and chastised Spanish ineptness that had contributed to the Seminoles' autonomy.[51] In military activities subsequent to the Patriots War, Spanish Governor Mauricio de Zuniga informed the American commander, General Andrew Jackson, that the runaways, "[a]s rational beings, may be subjects of the king, my master, [and] are deemed by me insurgents or rebels against the authority, not only of his Catholic Majesty, but also of the proprietors for whose service they have withdrawn themselves."[52]

After more than three centuries of dominance in the Western Hemisphere, the Spanish Empire was falling. With more important colonies in revolt, Spain had no desire to challenge the ascending

United States. Just subsequent to the Patriots War, U.S. forces led by General Jackson made a special effort to capture or destroy Spain's African rebel allies in the First Seminole War.[53]

Jackson's campaign failed to capture rebel warriors, but a few non-combatants were taken. As a consequence of the Spanish weakness and the relative strength of the Seminoles, President Monroe notified Congress in his State of the Union Address that he was pressuring Spain to relinquish Florida, partially as a quid pro quo for millions of dollars in slave property that had found refuge there for decades.[54]

According to Monroe, Spain had not abided by the tenets of the 1795 Treaty of San Lorenzo, which required the return of runaways in Florida. Spain would indemnify the U.S. government. The government would indemnify the slave masters.[55]

Notes

1. Tyler, *American Nation*, 6.

2. Ibid., 9–30; Bailey, *American Pageant*, 12–13.

3. Bailey, *American Pageant*, 14.

4. Charlton W. Tebeau, *A History of Florida* (Coral Gables, Fla.: University of Miami Press, 1971), 43–55.

5. Gatscket, *Legend*, 64, 65; Joseph B. Smith, *The Plot to Steal Florida* (New York: Harbor House, 1983), 211, 255.

6. Landers, "African Presence," 321.

7. Alexander S. Salley Jr., ed., *Narratives of Early Carolina, 1650–1708* (New York: Charles Scribner's Sons, 1910), 122; Public Record Office, "America and the West Indies," vol. 11, 16.

8. Eugene M. Sirmans, *Colonial South Carolina: A Political History, 1663–1763* (Chapel Hill, N.C.: University of North Carolina Press, 1966), 23.

9. Salley, *Narratives*, 332–40.

10. Covington, *Seminoles of Florida*, 3–4; Sturtevant, "Creek," 92; Mulroy, *Border*, 6.

11. Salley, *Narratives*, 134.

12. Public Record Office, "America and the West Indies," vol. 10, 524–26.

13. David H. Corkran, *The Creek Frontier, 1540–1783* (Norman, Okla.: University of Oklahoma Press, 1967), 53, 57; Sturtevant, "Creek," 100.

14. Salley, *Narratives*, 332.

15. Public Record Office, "America and the West Indies," vol. 13, 187.

16. Wright, "Spanish Resistance," 141.

17. Salley, *Narratives*, 205; Public Record Office, "America and the West Indies," vol. 17, 104–7; Landers, "Free Town," 9–30.

18. Irene A. Wright, ed., "Dispatches of Spanish Officials Bearing on the Free Negro Settlement of Gracia Real de Santa Teresa de Mose, Florida," *The Journal of Negro History* 9 (1924): 144–95. Author's translation.

19. Landers, "Free Town," 11.

20. Charles II, *Royal Edict of 1693* (Gainesville, Fla.: John B. Stetson Collection, P. K. Yonge Library of Florida History, University of Florida, text-fiche), SD58–1–26.

21. Wright, "Dispatches," 156.

22. Salley, *Narratives*, 205.

23. Landers, "Free Town," 15, note 29.

24. Sturtevant, "Creek," 101; Corkran, *Creek Frontier*, 56–60; Public Record Office, "America and the West Indies," vol. 28, 299–300.

25. Landers, "Free Town," 15.

26. Ibid., 17; Landers explains in the text of note 38.

27. Public Record Office, "America and the West Indies," vol. 28, 227.

28. Ibid., 215–26.

29. J. H. Easterby, ed., *The Colonial Records of South Carolina: The Journal of the Commons House of Assembly*, vol. 1, 1736–1739 (Columbia, S.C.: Historical Commission of South Carolina, 1951), 590–96, 673–708.

30. Wright, "Dispatches," 164.

31. Ibid., 164, 173, 175.

32. The Mandingos were a key tribe of the Great Mali Empire located in West Africa from approximately AD 1100–1400. They were at the forefront of African continental resistance to European conquest. E. Jefferson Murphy, *History of African Civilization* (New York: Crowell, 1972), 114–22, 262–66, 308–10.

33. Ibid., 176; Landers, "African Presence," 321–22; Landers, "Free Town," 15–19.

34. Wright, "Dispatches," 173–76.

35. Ibid., 176.

36. J. H. Easterby, ed., *The Colonial Records of South Carolina: The Journal of the Commons House of Assembly*, vol. 3, 1741–1742 (Columbia, S.C.: The Historical Commission of South Carolina, 1953), 86–92.

37. Ibid., 87.

38. Ibid., 87–120.

39. Landers, "Free Town," 18–25.

40. Wright, "Dispatches," 193.

41. Ibid., 195.

42. Bailey, *American Pageant*, 59.

43. Ibid.

44. John Jay, *The Correspondence and Public Papers of John Jay, 1782–1793*, vol. 3, ed., Henry P. Johnson (New York: J. P. Putnam's Sons, 1891), 259, 357.

45. Smith, *Plot*, 112–15.

46. Ibid., 188–89.

47. Ibid., 244–69.

48. Covington, *Seminoles of Florida*, 28.

49. Smith, *Plot*, 211–12.

50. James Monroe, *The Writings of James Monroe, 1807–1816*, vol. 6 (New York: AMS Press, 1969), 62–79.

51. Ibid., 54–56.

52. Ibid., 62–79.

53. *Am. St. P.*, 1, *Foreign Relations*, 4:556.

54. President Monroe gives a State of the Union Address to both houses of Congress. *Annals of Congress*, 15th Cong., 2d sess., January 1820, 2037; Giddings, *Exiles*, 38.

55. President Monroe, "State of the Union Address to Congress," in *Annals of Congress*, 15th Cong., 2d sess., vol. 3, 2037; David Hunter Miller, ed., *Treaties and Other International Acts of the United States of America*, vol. 2, 1776–1818 (Washington, D.C.: U.S. Government Printing Office, 1931), 3–12, 318–23.

Section B

British and U.S. Initiatives against the Seminoles

In chapters 4, 5, and 6, we learn how first the British, then later, the U.S. political and military leaders reacted to the policies initiated by Spain, discussed in section A. In some cases, we discuss the same events mentioned in section A. However, this time we get a British or U.S. institutional and administrative perspective, which is necessary to have a clearly demarcated view of the political activities of the Spanish, British, and U.S. administrative structures.

In this section, British, and later American, policy-makers first seek diplomatic solutions to the problem of their slaves being accommodated in Florida. But when diplomacy fails, both nations eventually seek military remedies. The presence of rebel slaves in Florida limited the development and growth of British colonialism in the Southeast. It also interfered with the growth of the U.S. slave industry and exacerbated existing political problems in both nations.

Chapter 4

British Colonial Politics and the Florida Rebels, 1693–1763

During the 17th century the British began to settle the North American continent. The African slave industry evolved into the economic foundation of this colonization effort. This evolution was overwhelmingly true in the plantation economies of Maryland, Virginia, and the Carolinas. The southern Carolinians initially thrived on an Indian slave industry, although African slavery existed simultaneously. However, in general, the colonists depended most on the Africans.

The London proprietors who held the founding charter of the Carolina colony wanted the colonists to be financially self-reliant as soon as possible. They needed to expand acreage, plant, clear, and settle. African slaves facilitated their settlement. However, as slaves ran away to Florida and became allies of the Spanish, the British colonization effort in Carolina was jeopardized. Between 1693 and 1763, the blacks, natives, and Spanish kept the colonies of the Southeast on the defensive, which formed the basis for the political relationship between the British and the rebels. The political activities and policies of officials often were directly or indirectly reactions to the rebel presence. The British first responded to the rebels diplomatically; after diplomacy failed, they attempted a military solution. Within the framework of this two-step process, various political activities occurred that demonstrated the nature of the relationship between the British and the rebels. Ultimately, the rebels would help the Spanish achieve their goal of slowing down and even reversing the development and expansion of the British colonial effort in the Southeast.

By 1662, King Charles II had granted a charter to eight proprietors to establish the colony of Carolina. These men were politicians who sought to profit by overseas investments. By 1665, Charles II extended the boundaries of the Carolina colony all the way to St. Augustine. Until this time, Spain had not officially acknowledged the presence of the British in North America on land claimed by Spain. But shortly after this extension, the Spaniards accepted the presence of Britain as far south as what would become Charleston.[1] The proprietors had invested much of their own money in Carolina. To ensure returns on their investments and the overall safety and prosperity of the colony, they needed peaceful relations with the natives and with Spain. However, instead of leaving the British to peacefully develop Carolina, Spain launched attacks on their settlements. From St. Augustine, they enlisted the help of their native allies, the Apalachees.

The British charter granted the proprietors extensive control over the colony: They controlled all royalties and privileges, they made laws and wrote the colony's constitution with the advice of colonial freemen under conditions that they set, and they appointed a governor and determined the manner in which the legislative body and all administrators would be selected.[2] Ultimately, the proprietors and colonial politicians were forced to react to the Spanish attacks and the resulting impact on Carolina's development. By 1670, Governor William Sayles had notified the proprietors that the Carolina militia and its Creek allies were battling the Spanish and their Apalachee allies.[3] It is difficult to say with certainty, but either the proprietors or the colonial politicians initiated a policy of enslaving the natives who were allies of the Spanish in Florida. This move resulted in a prosperous "Indian slave trade." Also, the Creeks supplied the British with thousands of deerskins. The Carolina colonists involved with enslaving natives were the first to prosper. This Indian trade had the dual benefits of generating profits and eliminating the chief ally of the Spanish. These Indian slaves were generally sold out of Carolina to the West Indies.[4]

In 1674, Dr. Henry Woodward wrote to a proprietor, the earl of Shaftesbury, regarding the initiation of native slavery: "Very well satisfied, dispatched [members of the Savannah tribe] homewards that evening, whom I again expect in March with deerskins, furs and young slaves."[5]

On another occasion in 1680, the proprietors instructed the governor and council of Carolina to set up a board for handling disputes between colonists and Indians and stated that no friendly Indians were to be enslaved or sold out of the colony.[6] Such comments indicate that the proprietors may have approved of the trade, were notified of its beginning, and later distinguished between natives who were to be enslaved and those who were not. On other occasions, however, the proprietors seem to blame colonial politicans for the dualistic Indian trade. In 1684 in a letter to the Carolina governor, the proprietors wrote: "Some evil men have of late made a trade of enslaving and sending away the poor Indians, for which purpose unjust wars have been made on them.... We did not mean... the parliament should license the transporting of Indians bought of other Indians... for it is only an encouragement to keep those poor people at war with each other."[7]

This comment from the proprietors indicates that somehow the trade was initiated, regulated, and controlled by the colonists. At any rate, it was an integral part of the economy and seemed to bolster Carolina's defense strategy. Carolina's political leaders prospered and competed for control of the lucrative trade. In the process, some were removed from power by the proprietors specifically for engaging in the trade.[8] Vigorous pursuit of the trade, according to John Oldmixon, was the sole reason for Governor Moore's entering politics. Oldmixon says Moore rigged legislative elections and even allowed mulattos and blacks to vote. In 1702, Moore finally launched a slave-catching expedition against St. Augustine in the guise of an offensive war.[9]

The efforts of the Carolina politicians resulted in the near extermination of the Apalachees, which was a setback for Spain.[10] Whether the trade was sanctioned by the proprietors or not, this two-track policy worked in the interest of Britain, extending prosperity and growth, and eliminating an ally of its enemy. From another perspective, though, the policy contributed to the future instability in Carolina. Apalachees who were fortunate enough to escape from the British perhaps naturally went back to Florida. Before 1700, Carolina had an African slave population at least four times as great as its white population. It seems that African and Indian slaves fled slavery together and went to Florida.[11] Carolinian Edward Randolph notified Parliament that in 1686 a Spanish invasion force included natives and blacks. They had carried away 13 slaves and refused to return them.[12] In response, by 1689 the proprietors notified Governor Seth Sothell, "[Y]ou must take care to prevent servants and [b]lacks from running away to the Spanish at St. Augustine." [13]

The zealous exploitation of the Indian slave trade effectively neutralized the Apalachee as military allies of the Spanish and physically placed them in the Carolina colony. Oppressed Indians and blacks were naturally opposed to serving as the foundation of the British colonial development strategy, and as oppressed people, they were natural allies. Their presence in Carolina as slaves was indeed initially positive for colonial expansion. However, the Apalachees had played a significant part in the Spanish effort to destabilize the British Southeast colonial effort. Consequently, perhaps they were also at the core of the British economic, political, and military initiatives in the region. The African slave industry in Carolina, if not equally important initially, certainly contributed the balance to the economic foundation of the colonies. When the Apalachees fled slavery and returned to Florida, they were accompanied by Africans. Therefore, the loss of valuable property and labor was doubled. [14]

The Spanish Edict of 1693 would drastically destabilize African slavery in the Southeast. However, the Yamasee War, 1714–16, would for all practical purposes destroy the "Indian trade." [15] The Yamasee War was perhaps the most critical event in the history of colonial southern Carolina. It inaugurated a period of formal reaction to the African, native, and Spanish assaults on the colony. Before 1714, nothing quite so alarming and destabilizing to the colony had occurred; the British had seemed to be on the offensive more than on the defensive. Colonial development and expansion had never been so threatened. This new challenge came directly as a result of native and African runaways rebelling against their role in the British economy.

In 1715, Lieutenant Governor Alexander Spotswood of Virginia wrote James Stanhope, secretary of state for the Southern Province, seeking military assistance and telling him that southern Carolina faced the greatest army of natives assembled since the English had arrived. He said that the natives were encouraged by Spain. A very dismal set of circumstances was projected. Spotswood questioned whether southern Carolina would survive because, he said, 1,500 white men were talking of leaving. The Carolina proprietors sought money and weapons from Parliament and asked for help from all other colonies. Parliament wanted to know how the proprietors would pay back the money, whether they would surrender their charter to the king, and whether they would be self-supporting in the future. The proprietors responded that this was the first time in 50 years that they had requested support from the king.[16]

Though Lieutenant Governor Spotswood had spoken in the heat of war, modern reflection reveals that the colony truly was in a crisis. Never before had there been such cause for alarm. Besides the questioning of their charter, perhaps the most telling comment is the proprietors' statement that they had never before had to request money from the king. The request for aid from other colonies also reveals the state of desperation that the political leaders of Carolina felt themselves to be in. Clearly, these comments by Spotswood demonstrate that the colony's development was severely at risk.[17]

After the Yamasee War, the Carolina proprietors and colonial politicians were able to make a good general assessment of how they were affected. By this time, they had gained some perspective on the 1693 edict and its overall impact on colonial development. In 1716, Joseph Boone and Richard Beresford, agents for the Carolina House of Commons, wrote to Parliament. They first pointed out that the governor of Virginia had done too little to assist Carolina and implied that military assistance might not be so eagerly extended to Virginia in a similar emergency. They said that unless London sent help, the colony would have to be abandoned and that the Spanish believed that they would soon capture Carolina. Boone and Beresford also said that because of the nearness of hostile forces, the abandoned plantations could not be resettled.[18]

Parallel to their political reaction to the war in general, the Carolinians complained about their great loss of Africans to the Spanish. They sent Major James Cockrane to St. Augustine to negotiate for the return of slaves. The Carolina assembly reported that the Spanish had a policy of granting freedom to all English slaves who arrived in Florida, and they revealed numerous affidavits from individuals who observed the Spaniards arming and sheltering the Carolina runaways. Boone told the proprietors that the Spanish governor had said that without the king's order he could not release British slaves who had become Catholic. Carolina Governor Robert Johnson reported to Parliament an unsuccessful attack on St. Augustine in 1719 for the purpose of recovering slaves. In 1716, the Carolina Committee of Assembly expressed the belief that the Spanish were repaying the British for what the British did to Spain's "Indian allies."[19]

For a decade following the Yamasee War, the British struggled to defend themselves from the constant attacks by the combined Florida forces. What had once been a thriving two-track policy for British colonial development now was on the verge of setting Carolinian development back 50 years. The native slave trade came to a virtual standstill in the years after the Yamasee War, and the African slave industry grew at a fantastic rate. According to one estimate, within 15 years after the end of the Yamasee War, South Carolina had only 2,500 white men capable of bearing arms and an ever-increasing slave population of more than 40,000.[20] Carolina's two-track development cycle yielded profits and development, and struck a blow at Spain, but a corollary of that cycle was rebellion. The king of Spain quickly moved to use the runaway British slaves, perhaps to fill military slots vacated by their almost extinct Apalachee allies. All these changes were to the utter horror of Carolina proprietors and colonial politicians.

By 1728, the Carolina colony had split into North and South Carolina. South Carolina Assembly President Arthur Middleton wrote to the British foreign minister, Holles Pelham, duke of Newcastle:

> I am sorry we are obliged so often to represent to the government the difficulty we labor under, from the new situation of St. Augustine to this place who, without any regard to peace or war, do continually annoy our southern frontiers.... We formerly complained of their receiving and harboring all our runaway Blacks, but since then, they have found out a new way of sending our own slaves against us, to rob and plunder us.... We are not only at a vast expense in guarding our Southern frontiers but the inhabitants are continually alarmed, and have no leisure to look after their crops. The Indians they send against us are sent out in small parties headed by two, three or more Spaniards and sometimes joined with Blacks, and all mischief they do is on a sudden, and by surprise, and the moment they have done it, they retire again to St. Augustine...so that our plantations, being all scattering, before any men can be got together, the robbers are fled, this trade they have followed for twenty years.[21]

In addition to attacks on land, the Spanish government of Florida equipped a fleet of small ships manned by Spaniards, blacks, and natives. This naval force, known as the Coast Guardes, launched destructive raids on British coastal settlements in Carolina and later in Georgia. The governor insisted that the ships could not be launched without the participation of the black rebels.[22] South Carolina officials clearly believed that their survival was at stake. If Spain's goal was to limit the development of British colonization in the Southeast, then it seems that it was successful in the years following the Yamasee War. Middleton's letter indicates that the 1693 edict facilitated the flow of runaways into Florida, swelling the Spanish forces. This situation resulted in vast military expenses for a now struggling colony, and not only halted the frontiers of settlement, but also caused their retraction. Even those settlers who continued to inhabit their land found that their production was crippled by the threat of attacks from St. Augustine. According to Middleton, such threats had been the case since before the Yamasee War.

The proprietors and colonial administrators were put in a defensive or reactive posture. To the extent that their development strategy depended on slavery, it was failing. They talked of abandoning the colony. Diplomatic overtures to St. Augustine were unsuccessful. Therefore, it seems that expansion of the colony was no longer an issue, only its very survival. Also, to the degree that runaway Africans bolstered Spain's military power, it seems that South Carolina now targeted those slaves in a manner similar to its former concentration on the Apalachees. The South Carolina government signed treaties with the Creeks and Cherokees in which the natives were to be paid a bounty for live runaways or a lesser amount for each scalp.

However, South Carolina's primary reaction to St. Augustine was to intensify its own military effort. A major British military assault came in 1728. Colonel John Palmer attacked St. Augustine by land, and Captain Thomas Mounjoy, by sea, but neither invasion by South Carolina was successful. Furthermore, Palmer's lack of success was ensured by the strong effort of a black militia led by South Carolina runaways. The Carolina assembly blamed Palmer's failure on a lack of support from London. In communications with the proprietors, the assembly said that Palmer did not have proper orders for attacking St. Augustine Fort.[23]

In the wake of Palmer's unsuccessful raid, an air of frustration could be detected in communications between London and Charleston. As plans were being made to launch some strikes on Spanish colonies in the West Indies, the Carolinas were seen as not being available: "We must not hope for much assistance from either of the Carolinas; I believe the Spaniards will probably find them business enough at home; a proclamation lately published at St. Augustine has drawn many of their Blacks from them, in hopes of being enfranchised; and the rest are ripe for rebellion; so that it is really now come to pass that either the people of Carolina must take St. Augustine or St. Augustine will take them."[24]

The efforts of the Carolinians to use the military to achieve political policy had not been successful. London officials seemed to have contemplated making some military strikes against the Spanish. However, those plans apparently did not include an invasion of Florida commensurate with the goals of the South Carolinians. Being unable to dislodge the Spaniards, retrieve runaway slaves, or curtail the guerrilla strikes by force or diplomacy prompted Charleston and London to take other action.

As early as 1716, Carolina assembly agents Boone and Beresford notified Parliament that one way to encourage strength and development was to allow settlement on the Yamasee lands between Florida and Carolina. However, in the same letter they added, "But we cannot expect that any person will come to settle there 'till the Yamasees be removed from Augustine." By 1716, the assembly did pass an act encouraging settlement on Yamasee lands for defensive purposes. However, by 1718, the proprietors repealed this assembly act.[25] The proprietors probably believed that, in the wake of the war, confiscation and settlement of Yamasee lands could reignite intensive warfare.

It seems that between 1718 and 1728, consistent depredations by St. Augustine and the failure of Colonel Palmer's invasion helped to convince London that a change of policy was needed. Within two years of Palmer's invasion, James Oglethorpe proposed to establish a new colony that would incorporate the Yamasee lands. He suggested that Georgia be established as a fortification between Florida and South Carolina under the command of the South Carolina governor.[26]

James Oglethorpe was one of several trustees granted a charter for the establishment of the colony of Georgia in 1732. In *Some Account of the Design of the Trustees for Establishing Colonies in America*, Oglethorpe explained the purpose of the new colony. He said that before the Yamasee War, English settlers lived dispersed among natives as though the country were a conquered nation, but after the war all settlements were moved north of the Edisto River. The region south of Edisto and Port Royal, Oglethorpe wrote, would be the Georgias.[27]

As Oglethorpe took measure of the prevailing political-military predicament between Britain and Spain in the Southeast, he suggested the following: "The District intended for a new colony whilst it lies uninhabited will facilitate the Invasions of the Indians upon South Carolina. But a number of towns established along the Rivers Savannah and Alatamaha would prevent any future massacre and make a stronger barrier to the present settlements and keep the Negro Slaves of South Carolina in awe who are now so numerous as to be dreadful even to their masters."[28]

Also, the Georgia charter forbade slavery or even the presence of blacks. The proprietors reasoned that any blacks spotted could be apprehended as runaways from South Carolina or as soldiers of St. Augustine. Boone and Beresford had previously recommended settlement of the Yamasee lands. The success of the Florida allies seems to have convinced the political leaders in London that this was a good strategy. Oglethorpe had been elected to the House of Commons at age 26 in 1722. Because some of the South Carolina trustees were also members of the House of Commons, he was well aware of their defense needs. But it seems that Oglethorpe's desire to shield South Carolina was secondary. In 1728, a friend of his, who was an architect, was sent to debtors' prison, where he died of smallpox. Oglethorpe responded by conducting a parliamentary investigation into unhealthful conditions in debtors' prisons. His investigation led to the release from prison of more than 10,000 debtors. By 1730, he and other London humanitarians had petitioned the king for a charter to set up a charity colony. In 1732, the charter was granted. All trustees for Georgia were forbidden from owning land in the colony or profiting from office.[29]

Oglethorpe arrived in Charleston in 1733. Though aware of his mission to fortify the South Carolina frontier, he seems to have been more concerned about his philanthropic effort. However, from the beginning, Governor Johnson of South Carolina made certain that the colonists realized their place in the military strategy of the region. He forbade any colonist other than Oglethorpe from disembarking in Charleston for fear of the colonists not wanting to go on to the challenges of Georgia.[30]

Even as the Georgia colony was being established, there was no relief for South Carolina. In the mid-1730s, the South Carolina assembly stated that slave desertions were directly caused by the Spanish policy of granting freedom to all South Carolina slaves. One South Carolina slaveholder, Captain Caleb Davis, wrote to the assembly saying that 19 of his slaves and 50 belonging to other Port Royal planters had run off to St. Augustine. Davis went to St. Augustine and demanded that the governor return the slaves. But the governor informed Davis that he was commanded by the king to free the English slaves. Davis recommended that London send a high official to negotiate with Spain. A joint committee was set up to deal with desertions.[31]

The committee decided that the Spanish encouragement of slave deserters and their incorporation into the guerrilla militia of St. Augustine would have "fatal consequences to the safety and welfare of the province."[32] The committee's continued offer of rewards to Creeks for the capture of slaves proved ineffective. The assembly notified London that South Carolina would not survive unless the king acted to negotiate Spain's violations of existing treaties or provided military assistance. Additionally, the Spanish Edict of 1693 had been distributed throughout South Carolina. The House of Commons determined in 1739 that no efforts attempted against St. Augustine had been successful.[33]

A considerable quantity of correspondence between the South Carolina government and Parliament dealt with St. Augustine. Many of the South Carolina colonial records of the time were concerned with the same problem. The colonial political leaders believed that only military force could prevent the Spaniards from destroying their colony. The founding of Georgia was indeed a calculated military gesture, but even this change was proving to have no effect on the prevention of runaways and Spanish aggression.

James Oglethorpe maintained his seat in Parliament until 1743, even though he was in Georgia. During this time, as a member of the House of Commons and as a proprietor in the Georgia colony, he continually informed both bodies of the progress of the colony. John Perceval, the earl of Egmont (the first president of the Georgia Board of Trustees), received the following correspondence from Oglethorpe:

> On the 10th November, 1738, Colonel Oglethorpe wrote me the disagreeable situation he was in, a great number of debts, empty magazine, no money to supply them, numbers of people to be fed, mutinous soldiers to command, a Spanish claim, and a large body of their troops not far from him. That debt could not be avoided, since no one could dare dismiss the militia, or reduce the garrisons 'till the King's troops arrived to relieve them: and this had forced an expense of 20,000 pounds in a year, when only 8,000 pounds was granted . . . there must be a vigorous application to Parliament to pay those debts.[34]

Even though Georgia was chartered in part as a defensive barrier between Florida and South Carolina, it seems that the proprietors underestimated just how extensive the military expenditures would be. By 1738, the colony's expenses were almost 300 percent higher than had been projected. Because Georgia was chartered on a non-profit basis, Parliament was more directly involved in its fate and its role in the struggle with Spanish Florida.

Many Georgia colonists consistently complained to London because slavery was prohibited. As a result of these complaints, numerous efforts were made to remind the proprietors of the critical role slavery would have in Georgia. In 1739, Robert Williams wrote the earl of Egmont about a request for slaves. He said it would "ruin the colony, it being impossible to prevent Blacks deserting to the Spaniards our near neighbors, who give freedom, land, and protection to all runaway Blacks."[35] The issues of defense and the request for slaves seem to have been the dominant issues of correspondence between Georgia and London. Georgia proprietors not only had to develop a strategy for coping with St. Augustine, but also had to battle fellow members of Parliament, essentially because of the high defense expenditures. One leading member of Parliament, Sir Robert Walpole, questioned Georgia's annual budget overruns because he assumed the current treaty between Spain and England would be sufficient to keep the peace. Bills for defense expenditures, boats, and other essentials regularly arrived in London from Georgia. One parliamentarian, Thomas Towers, a trustee, believed there would be peace with Spain if the Georgia-Florida border were moved north, because he said there was no legitimate English title to the colony. In response to Towers, the earl of Egmont said that perhaps Parliament would vote for additional aid if the proprietors could forge a title.[36]

In 1738 and 1739, the lifeline between Georgia and London consisted of defense expenditures. A scandal occurred in 1739 when the Georgia recordskeeper, Thomas Causton, was accused of improper expenditures, but Causton blamed all of the cost overruns on defense needs. In 1739, the trustees collected records from Oglethorpe and requested more. Copies were made for each trustee in London for the purpose of lobbying Parliament to approve additional expenditures for Georgia. Sir Robert Walpole was seen as an enemy of the colony. He believed that England did not have a legal title and that in the current round of treaty negotiations it was likely that Spain could present a legitimate title. Many in Parliament believed it was futile to spend so much to back a lost cause. However, the trustees promised to vote against the interests of those members who abandoned Georgia. The earl of Egmont lobbied both houses of Parliament, winning the influential support of Lord Baltimore and the earl of Chesterfield. Finally, Walpole announced that he had secured the king's consent for money and fortifications for Georgia, while Lord Bathhurst declared that the king would rather part with the Indies than with Georgia. In response, Georgia trustee Robert Tracey announced that the Spanish minister to England, Giraldini, informed him that the king of Spain would rather part with Madrid than with Georgia and that the Spanish would fight England for 20 years before letting go of Georgia.[37]

In general, the Georgia trustees and colonial politicians were fighting against Spanish interests and the interests of macro-rebellion. The colony was conceived as a defensive barrier to those allied interests. However, the colonial charter's structure required dependency on Parliament. Georgia's quest to confront the external enemy in Florida, therefore, required confrontations with internal foes in Parliament to secure defense expenditures. Political diplomacy was conducted between London and Madrid as well as with Charleston, Savannah, and St. Augustine. Diplomacy had its limits, however: Spain and Britain finally decided that war would be the political determinant in their colonial competition. The conflict had reached the highest levels of government. The Spanish were prepared to fight for 20 years, and the king of England ordered defensive preparations for Georgia.

In 1739, a diplomatic mission from St. Augustine made several stops in Georgia and South Carolina. However, colonial officials of those colonies decided that St. Augustine was using this cover of diplomacy to shield its true mission. Oglethorpe arrested the party and charged its members with spreading news of a new 1733 Spanish edict of freedom and with inciting slaves to run to Florida and rebel. The Stono Rebellion of 1739 was blamed on this group. This rebellion, which occurred in South Carolina, resulted in the deaths of dozens of whites and blacks. The new edict and the rebellion that it incited were considered to be unpardonable crimes and prompted the colonists of Georgia and South Carolina to seek a declaration of war from their king.[38]

Oglethorpe informed the earl of Egmont that he had received the king's command to attack St. Augustine and that he would need additional expenditures to pay for the allegiance of 1,200 Creeks and Cherokees. He added that he had to strike before reinforcements arrived in St. Augustine from Havana, because Georgia and South Carolina had more troops than St. Augustine. He reminded Egmont, "[I]t is impossible to keep the province of Carolina without destroying Augustine, or keeping rangers and scout boats to restrain their nimble parties."[39]

Oglethorpe went before the South Carolina legislature as the commander of what became known as the "War of Jenkins' Ear." This war got its name from an incident in which Robert Jenkins, an English pirate, had his ship seized and his ear severed by a Spanish captain in the West Indies. In 1739, Jenkins held up his ear in Parliament to help spur a vote for war with Spain.[40]

In an address to the legislature, Oglethorpe reminded the South Carolina assembly of the king's orders to destroy St. Augustine. He said St. Augustine was the source of refuge for murderous bands of runaway slaves who, with Spanish and Indian allies, plundered British southeast colonies.[41]

Most of the military supplies and expenditures were supplied by the South Carolina legislature. However, support for the campaign arrived from as far away as Rhode Island. Oglethorpe marched to St. Augustine with 2,000 Indians, 2,200 white troops, and black laborers with additional whites to guard them. The expedition cost 120,000 pounds, but South Carolinians determined they could save 10,000 pounds annually in defense if the mission succeeded. Men and ships arrived from England to complete a seven-ship blockade of St. Augustine.[42]

St. Augustine was a large fort with thick walls and a moat. According to Captain Mark Carr, it was the only place of strength in Florida. He said it had 50 cannons and could house all the inhabitants of Florida. Carr noted that within one league of the fort was a village of 200 armed blacks and nine villages of Indians with 500 armed men.[43] Oglethorpe was unable to bombard St. Augustine into submission. The only route to a land invasion was through Fort Mose. Mose was constructed and inhabited by escaped Carolina slaves for the specific purpose of shielding St. Augustine from invasions.

When Oglethorpe arrived at Mose, he found it deserted. He ordered Colonel Vander Dussen and Captain Palmer to occupy Mose while he proceeded to lay siege to St. Augustine. On June 15, at four 4 A.M., Palmer and Dussen were hit with a surprise attack by 300 blacks and Indians. Killed in the attack were 80 British soldiers, and 25 were taken prisoner: Almost half of the British troops in the Fort Mose attack survived by running into the surrounding forest and swamps, but Colonel Dussen was mortally wounded. The blacks and Indians reoccupied Mose until June 30, then again vanished into the forest.

After suffering these losses, Oglethorpe dispersed his troops, but he did not attempt a frontal assault on St. Augustine. British forces all feared that the black and Indian forces would surprise them with guerrilla attacks. The British naval blockade had to be lifted because of bad weather. Therefore, the bombardment of St. Augustine by land and sea proved insufficient to induce a Spanish capitulation, and with the black and Indian guerrillas at their backs, Oglethorpe evacuated his forces on July 5.[44]

Other than the casualties at Fort Mose, the British forces sustained few deaths, but the losses at Mose demoralized them. Some of the Mose corpses were decapitated, and others were mutilated. The South Carolina Assembly appointed a special committee to investigate the result of the campaign. Their published account, "Report of the Committee Appointed to Inquire into the Causes of the Disappointment of Success in the Late Expedition against St. Augustine," revealed that the British were defeated by numerically inferior forces. The committee determined that white Spanish forces never left the St. Augustine fort and that only blacks and Indians had attacked the British on the ground. Oglethorpe reported that British forces at Fort Mose were lost only because they disobeyed his orders.[45]

Frequently, the official correspondence between Charleston, Savannah, and London expressed the belief that British colonial expansion and stabilization in South Carolina and Georgia demanded the conquest of St. Augustine. The British government had amassed one of the largest European armies ever seen in North America up to that time. The military conflict with St. Augustine not only forced the proprietors and colonists to respond militarily and increase defense expenditures, but also sparked intra-parliamentary confrontations over Georgia's survival.

Oglethorpe's campaign in Florida perhaps cannot be called a defeat because, other than the major battle at Fort Mose, there were very few real battles. The Spanish did not leave St. Augustine, and after the Fort Mose attack, the blacks and Indians primarily remained out of sight. But Oglethorpe's lack of success seems to be most important politically. The proprietors and colonial politicians were still faced with a powerful, even rejuvenated, foe in St. Augustine, now ready for revenge. Also, Georgia's parliamentary foes had to be confronted.

Before Oglethorpe's defeat, the earl of Egmont believed that the War of Jenkins' Ear provided a good opportunity to gain full parliamentary endorsement of Georgia. He felt that a British victory would eclipse the Spanish claims and certainly secure additional funding, but defeat brought the intensification of Spanish attacks and continued destablization of South Carolina and Georgia. In 1741, Parliament reported that a Spanish force of more than 2,300 troops, including at least 800 black and Indian troops, was poised to invade South Carolina and Georgia.[46]

By 1742, a British prisoner, Alexander Perris, who had been held in St. Augustine since the War of Jenkins' Ear, gave a deposition to the South Carolina assembly. Perris reported that a Spanish force that included 500 blacks had just invaded South Carolina and Georgia. In "A Free Town in Spanish Colonial Florida," Jane Landers writes that in the decade following the War of Jenkins' Ear, St. Augustine sent militias of separate and combined groups of blacks and Indians into British territory. The black militia of Fort Mose was led by a South Carolina runaway, Captain Francisco Menendez. The blacks were sent into Georgia and South Carolina to arm slaves and prepare them for a Spanish counterattack following the War of Jenkins' Ear. Also, the Spanish launched numerous corsairs against the British coastal settlements in the 1740s.[47]

Though unsuccessful in 1740, Oglethorpe eventually managed to defend Georgia and perhaps fight the Spaniards to a draw. In 1741, Oglethorpe complained to the earl of Egmont that the Spanish corsairs "swarmed the Georgia coast," and he notified Sir Robert Walpole of his plans for a second invasion of Florida. In 1742, Oglethorpe led a second invasion of St. Augustine that had only limited success, but he managed to inflict extensive damage on the Spanish forces after retreating into Georgia and staging several defensive battles. The earl of Egmont reported that a 1742 Spanish force of 3,000 men was led by the governor of St. Augustine. In this attack, Oglethorpe defended Georgia on land and sea. As a result of his defensive maneuvers, Oglethorpe was promoted to the rank of general in 1743.[48]

The 1740s were a decade of intensive warfare between the British and Spanish in the Southeast. Both sides launched raids and counter-raids on each other. The Spanish were not able to push the British from Georgia, and the British could not conquer St. Augustine. It seems that the South Carolina political leaders began to give fewer accounts of Spanish penetration into their territory; to the extent that this is accurate, perhaps the strategy of making Georgia a barrier was starting to succeed. However, decreased penetration of South Carolina did not seem to limit criticism of the Georgia colony in Parliament, nor did Oglethorpe's apparent defensive success facilitate expansion or development of the colony. Oglethorpe's lack of success in the War of Jenkins' Ear seemed to bring a new source of conflict, this time in North America.

As Oglethorpe retreated in 1740, the earl of Egmont reported: "The Council and Assembly of South Carolina signed a petition and representation to His Majesty expressing their miserable condition, their apprehensions of the Spaniards, upon the ill success of ye siege of Augustine which they impute to Colonel Oglethorpe's bad conduct, their danger from their own Blacks, and that their expectations and hopes arising at first from the settlement of Georgia were now vanished and gone."[49]

The South Carolina assembly investigation reported that after the attack on the British at Fort Mose, the Creeks who had accompanied them into battle accused Oglethorpe of being afraid of the Spanish.[50] Lieutenant Colonel Cockrane reported after the war, "[I]n Carolina they cannot hear the name of Colonel Oglethorpe, but they fall into such a rage as sets the very dogs a barking."[51] The Carolinians' deaths at the hands of the blacks and Indians, in particular, probably contributed heavily to the South Carolina assembly's embitterment over the outcome in St. Augustine. Numerous survivors of the 1740 campaign criticized Oglethorpe's leadership. The South Carolina assembly even sent pamphlets to both houses of Parliament critical of Oglethorpe, but Governor James Glen of South Carolina managed to block their distribution. He feared it would discourage expenditures for a second expedition. Several members of Parliament requested that Governor Glen lead the next expedition. The enmity of the South Carolina assembly toward Oglethorpe was not based solely on words. Oglethorpe reported to the earl of Egmont and to the British foreign minister, the duke of Newcastle, in 1742 and 1743 respectively, that during major invasions from Florida, the South Carolina assembly refused to lend any assistance.[52]

The conflict with South Carolina seemed to have been only a limited corollary of the British confrontation with Spain and its allies. Nevertheless, it resulted from the continuous military instability in the region. The inability of Oglethorpe and other proprietors to resolve their development problems through war continued to provide their enemies in Parliament with the resources to attack the colony. In late 1740, the proprietors requested a 25 percent increase in the defense spending for Georgia. In the parliamentary debates that followed, several members requested that Georgia be abandoned because it was too expensive to defend. They proposed that the colonists join South Carolina and strengthen that colony. Lord Gage stated that he regretted having voted 129,000 pounds to Georgia. Thomas Christie argued that during this debate he had signed a petition to allow blacks in Georgia, but on learning of the Spanish edicts that freed British slaves, he and several others in Parliament would have preferred to wait until St. Augustine was conquered. Other members complained that parliamentary debates on Georgia only encouraged the Spaniards to attack.[53]

Though Georgia was founded partially as a haven for debt prisoners, the nature of parliamentary debates indicates that it was more important as a military barrier for South Carolina. The conflict between South Carolina and Georgia was rooted in military issues as well. The Spaniards used runaway Carolina slaves to limit Carolina's growth. Because the colony's growth depended on the slave industry, it was believed that Georgia would protect slavery and ensure growth. In fulfilling this defensive role for South Carolina, Georgia was a far more expensive project than was planned. As Parliament debated the cost-effectiveness of maintaining this garrison state, alternative funding sources had to be considered. The only real alternative was the introduction of slavery. Georgia's colonists insisted that the problems of hunger and trade could be solved only with slaves and that the colony could function as a garrison without inhabitants. Oglethorpe insisted that the St. Augustine attacks were designed to make Georgia too costly for Parliament, introduce slavery as an alternative funding source for the colony, and consequently provide a new source of rebel allies closer to Florida than to South Carolina. Also, he said that the Spaniards hoped to make Parliament grow tired of funding Georgia.[54]

While Parliament debated continued funding of Georgia, one of the colony's administrators, Thomas Stephens, sent the following comments: "Your chief aim is to introduce Blacks, but its demonstrable that is a thing not to be ventured. You say that without them no exportable commodities can be raised, why none ought to be expected yet. Georgia is a frontier province, and not to be considered yet a while as a region profitable in a commercial way, but as a garrison defense, and the inhabitants as soldiers with arms in their hands, not spades. But when rendered secure, then is the time for them to apply themselves to such produces."[55]

Stephens's comments shed light on the complex political reactions of colonial politicians to the military force from St. Augustine. Though Georgia was originally put in place to safeguard slavery in Carolina, the expense of this policy led to a demand for slavery in Georgia. The words of Oglethorpe and Stephens reflect a British colonial predicament in the Southeast: using slaves to secure development, but also furnishing the Spanish with handy guerrilla recruits.

Gradually, some members of Parliament accepted demands from colonists, who were influenced by the fiscal realities. They argued that Georgia must accept slavery or risk losing funds from Parliament.[56] Finally, in 1750, slavery was allowed in Georgia, but until that time the Parliament trustees and Georgia colonial leaders continued to debate the issues of slavery, development, and the Spanish encouragement of runaways. To the extent that several members of Parliament tired of the continued military expenditures, steps were taken to consolidate Georgia and South Carolina. By 1750, Parliament had even disbanded Oglethorpe's military regiment. The Georgia colonial government was instructed to direct its request for military assistance to the governor of South Carolina. Nevertheless, by 1752, Parliament had forced the trustees of Georgia to surrender their charter. By this time, slavery was allowed, and Parliament decided to keep troops in Georgia.[57]

In deciding to allow slavery in Georgia, Parliament and the trustees opted for the strategy of seeking development and minimizing the number of slaves escaping to St. Augustine. The records indicate that the St. Augustine forces continued to limit the extent of development and expansion. In 1752, the freeholders of southern Georgia reported increased Spanish attacks after the reduction in Oglethorpe's regiment.[58]

The conflict between Britain and Spain was dramatically altered in 1763. In that year, the Treaty of Paris gave Florida to the British. Spain, however, regained Florida in 1783 during the American Revolution. In 1763, Georgia Governor James Wright wrote to Parliament: "I most sincerely and heartily congratulate your lordships on the peace which his majesties wisdom and equity has so happily concluded . . . by the cessation of Florida, not only of the settlements of St. Augustine and Pensacola and now that your lordships are pleased to inform me that this province will be freed from every obstacle that has obstructed its growth and prosperity, and be no longer checked and cramped, I have no doubt of its making great strides, and very soon becoming useful to the mother country."[59]

Wright underscores the historical plight of Georgia's development. The Treaty of Paris had yielded an objective to the British that decades of war could not. Wright expressed optimism that the guerrilla attacks would cease. No longer would a Spanish edict draw British slaves to Florida. Nonetheless, in spite of the absence of the Spanish, Wright reported that by 1766 slaves still ran off to Florida. By 1771, the Georgia Assembly passed legislation designed to prevent slaves from becoming runaways. In the same year, Governor Wright reaffirmed agreements with the Upper Creeks to pay them for the capture of runaways.[60]

Notes

1. Alexander Hewatt, *History of South Carolina and Georgia*, vol. 1 (London: Alexander Donaldson, 1779), 42–45; Weir, *Colonial South Carolina*, 47–50.

2. Hewatt, *History*, 42–43.

3. Salley, *Narratives*, 122.

4. Ibid., 134; Corkran, *Creek Frontier*, 49–53; Daniel F. Littlefield Jr., *Africans and Creeks: From the Colonial Period to the Civil War* (Westport, Conn.: Greenwood Press, 1979), 5–6; Sirmans, *Colonial South Carolina*, 23–25.

5. Salley, *Narratives*, 134.

6. Public Record Office, "America and the West Indies," vol. 10, 524–26.

7. Ibid., vol. 11, 645.

8. Salley, *Narratives*, 328.

9. Ibid., 334–40.

10. Covington, *Seminoles of Florida*, 3–4.

11. Weir, *Colonial South Carolina*, 31.

12. Public Record Office, "America and the West Indies," vol. 17, 104–7.

13. Ibid., vol. 13, 187.

14. Landers, "African Presence," 321; Wright, "Dispatches," 144–93.

15. Landers, "African Presence," 321; Landers, "Free Town," 15; Public Record Office, "America and the West Indies," vol. 29, 227, 299–300.

16. Public Record Office, "America and the West Indies," vol. 28, 226–32.

17. Ibid.

18. Ibid., vol. 29, 215–21.

19. Ibid., vol. 30, 207, and vol. 28, 218.

20. Littlefield, *Africans and Creeks*, 9; James E. Oglethorpe, *Some Account of the Design of the Trustees for Establishing Colonies in America* (1732; reprint, ed. Rodney M. Baine and Phinizy Spalding, Athens, Ga.: University of Georgia Press, 1990), 14–22.

21. Public Record Office, "America and the West Indies," vol. 36, 131.

22. Ibid., 133; Easterby, *Colonial Records of South Carolina*, vol. 3, 291; Landers, "Free Town," 22.

23. Easterby, *Colonial Records of South Carolina*, vol. 3, 291; Public Record Office, "America and the West Indies," vol. 36, 134; Landers, "Free Town," 15.

24. Public Record Office, "America and the West Indies," vol. 36, 291.

25. Ibid., vol. 29, 220, and vol. 30, 322.

26. Ibid., vol. 37, 358, 385.

27. Oglethorpe, *Account of the Design*, 18–22, 129–30.

28. Ibid., 23.

29. Kenneth Coleman, *Colonial Georgia* (New York: Charles Scribner's Sons, 1976), 13–17; Merrill Jensen, ed., *English Historical Documents to 1776* (New York: Oxford University Press, 1962), 493–94.

30. Ibid., 24.

31. Easterby, *Colonial Records of South Carolina*, vol. 1, 590–97, 673.

32. Ibid., 673.

33. Ibid., 680–709.

34. John Perceval, "The Journal of the Earl of Egmont," in *The Colonial Records of Georgia*, vol. 5, ed. Allen D. Candler (Atlanta: Franklin-Turner, 1906), 74.

35. Ibid., 93.

36. Ibid., 97–108.

37. Ibid., 102, 115–47.

38. Ibid., 164–67; Easterby, *Colonial Records of South Carolina*, vol. 3, 83.

39. Perceval, "Journal," 231, 256; Easterby, *Colonial Records of South Carolina*, vol. 3, 83–85.

40. Herbert E. Bolton and Mary Ross, *The Debatable Land* (Berkeley, Calif.: University of California Press, 1925), 77–80.

41. Easterby, *The Colonial Records of South Carolina*, vol. 3, 87.

42. Ibid., 87–92; Perceval, "Journal," 229.

43. Perceval, "Journal," 293.

44. Easterby, *Colonial Records of South Carolina*, vol. 3, 100–36; Smith, *Plot*, 211.

45. Easterby, *Colonial Records of South Carolina*, vol. 3, 115, 116, 120, 147, 157, 194.

46. Perceval, "Journal," 280, 553.

47. Ibid., 553; Easterby, *Colonial Records of South Carolina*, vol. 3, 235; Landers, "Free Town," 21–25.

48. Perceval, "Journal," 525, 553, 611, 631.

49. Ibid., 394.

50. Easterby, *Colonial Records of South Carolina*, vol. 3, 119.

51. Perceval, "Journal," 499.

52. Ibid., 572, 645, 676.

53. Ibid., 413–14, 434, 491–99.

54. Ibid., 642.

55. Ibid., 440.

56. Ibid., 642.

57. Kenneth Coleman, ed., *Trustees Letter Book*, vol. 31, *Colonial Records of Georgia, 1745–1752* (Athens, Ga.: University of Georgia Press, 1986), 207, 254, 266.

58. Coleman and Ready, eds., "The Original Papers of Governor John Reynolds," vol. 27, 33, 47.

59. Kenneth Coleman and Milton Ready, eds., "The Original Papers of Governors Reynolds, Ellis, Wright, and Others," in *The Colonial Records of Georgia*, vol. 27, 1757–1763 (Athens, Ga.: University of Georgia Press, 1977), 445.

60. Ibid., 191, 342, 368.

Chapter 5

U.S. Reaction to the Black Seminoles, 1788–1814*

Between 1763 and 1783, British colonists went from being subjects of the crown to independent citizens of the United States of America. During those same years, Florida passed from the hands of the Spanish to those of the British and then back again. As a result, the political policies concerning runaway slaves varied from enforcement of the 1693 edict under the Spanish to nonenforcement under the British. During the American Revolution, the British encouraged Georgia slaves to run to Florida as potential allies. Because of this threat, the Georgia assembly required one-third of its militia to guard slaves.[1] Officially, however, British colonial Florida provided no haven for runaway slaves because slavery had increased since the end of Spanish occupation. During British occupation it seems likely that some of the black and Indian allies of the Spanish became incorporated among the Lower Creeks, who had migrated into Florida. The Lower Creeks, the rebels, the Apalachees, and the Yamasees all became known as the Seminoles during the British occupation.[2]

It was among the Seminoles that Georgia slaves found refuge after 1763. With the return of the Spanish occupation after the Revolution, runaways could have been received by the Spanish under terms of the

---

* See figure C on page 74.

Figure C – U.S. Political Policy and Black Seminoles

President	Political Policy	Impact of Policy		Relationship to MLR		Participant
		War	Peace	Direct	Indirect	
Washington	End of Edict of 1693–1790		X	X		Spain
Washington	Treaty of New York, 1790		X	X		Creek
Washington	Treaty of San Lorenzo, 1795		X	X		Spain
Madison	Patriots War, 1812–13	X			X	Spain and Seminole
Monroe	First Seminole War, 1817–18	X		X		Seminole
Monroe	Treaty of Washington, 1819		X	X		Spain
Monroe	Treaty of Indian Springs, 1821		X	X		Creek
Monroe	Treaty of Ft. Moultrie, 1823		X		X	Seminole
Jackson	Treaty of Payne's Landing, 1832		X		X	Seminole
Jackson	Second Seminole War, 1835–42	X		X		Seminole
Van Buren	Articles of Capitulation, 1837		X	X		Abraham/Black Seminole

1693 edict as well.[3] One factor that remained constant during both the Spanish and British occupation of Florida were the complaints of officials from Georgia. Rebel slaves were at the core of those complaints.

In this chapter we will discuss the political relationship between the Florida rebels and the U.S. government. In general, this relationship occurred within a framework of interaction already established by the British: First, the United States attempted diplomatic solutions, then military ones. In this context, I will show activities of and initiatives from politicians that demonstrate the political relationship. A key diplomatic effort culminated with the repeal of the Edicts of 1693 and 1733. The ultimate American initiative against the Florida threat was a secret war launched by James Madison.

With Britain's expansion into Florida in 1763, British colonial growth and development continued. Georgia's Governor Wright complained about runaways and made agreements with the Upper Creeks to capture them. It seems that in spite of British colonial expansion in Florida, runaways and Seminole attacks still hampered the colonies' growth. As early as 1785, a Georgia delegate to the Continental Congress, William Houston, served on a congressional committee that recommended to Congress ways to deal with the southern Indians. This committee suggested that U.S. Indian commissioners in Georgia be required to demand that Lower Creeks and Seminoles return all fugitive slaves who resided among them.[4]

Apparently, however, efforts by the commissioners did not result in the return of Georgia's slaves. By 1788, the Georgia governor and delegates pushed Congress to take stronger measures. They issued the following statement: "It is represented to Congress by the delegates of the State of Georgia that the . . . frontiers of that state have been for several years past invaded and kept in a state of alarm by Creek Indians . . . instigated by refugees and fugitive traders, who had formerly escaped from these states and taken refuge among them as to keep up constant and bloody incursions on the different parts of that frontier, and that the settlements of four of the exterior counties are almost entirely broken up."[5]

It is apparent that the attacks of the blacks and natives in the Georgia-Florida region limited the settlement of the state of Georgia. It is important to remember that the U.S. government acknowledged two groups of Creeks. The Upper Creeks resided primarily in Georgia and were the main body of the nation. They had been traditional allies of the British since before the Yamasee War, and Governor Wright paid them to capture runaway slaves. The Lower Creeks, who resided in Florida, generally became incorporated into a Seminole conglomerate. These were the notorious Creeks referred to by Congress. Here we see that the Seminoles were operating independently of the Spanish government in St. Augustine. Congress ordered the secretary of war to make plans for war against the Seminoles.[6]

From the Office of Foreign Affairs, Secretary of State John Jay reported in 1788 on the congressional statements. Jay noted that slaves from Georgia were escaping to St. Augustine and were being freed and sheltered by Florida Governor Vincente Zespedes. Jay reported that the governor said he could not return any slaves without orders from the king of Spain. As early as 1787, in a letter to Thomas Jefferson, Jay acknowledged that the Georgia frontier was under attack and implied that Spain should be punished. Jay also sent a letter to the U.S. envoy in Madrid, William Carmichael, instructing him to negotiate for an end to the Spanish policy of freeing and sheltering runaway slaves.[7]

For nearly a century, first the British, then the Americans, were forced to grapple with the effects of the Spanish Edict of 1693. This policy had been reasserted several times over the century. Its impact on colonial and U.S. expansion can be seen in the pattern of reaction by government officials. The policy bolstered the will of the Spanish militia in Florida. As a result, frontier settlements could be easily attacked. These attacks caused political reactions in Parliament and in the colonial assemblies of South Carolina and Georgia. Political responses later occurred in Georgia state politics and in the Continental Congress. Under the United States, efforts to obliterate the edict intensified.

As a member of the Continental Congress, James Madison made these comments:

> We learn from Georgia that the State is threatened with a dangerous war with the Creek Indians. The alarm is of so serious a nature that law martial has been proclaimed, and they are proceeding to fortify even the town of Savannah. The idea there is that the Indians derive their motives as well as their means from their Spanish neighbors. Individuals complain also that their fugitive slaves are encouraged by East Florida. The policy of this is explained by supposing that it is considered as a discouragement to the Georgians to form settlements near the Spanish boundaries.[8]

Madison clearly addresses the impact of the Seminoles and the Spanish on the expansion of the state of Georgia. He also makes reference to the natural reaction that echoed from many colonial political leaders. Madison's talk of war replicates the reactions of many legislative officials in former times. The Continental Congress pushed its Spanish envoy and the Florida governor for a repeal of the edict. As a congressional delegate, Madison was fully informed about the subject.

Under the new constitution of 1788, Thomas Jefferson replaced John Jay as secretary of state. By 1790, Jefferson continued to push Carmichael and the governor of Florida for changes in the Spanish policy. He sent transcripts and affidavits from Georgia slaveholders that had been received by Secretary of War Henry Knox. Jefferson told William Carmichael that the problems in Georgia were growing worse.[9] Finally, in 1790, Florida Governor Juan Quesada informed Jefferson that the king had rescinded the nearly century-old Edict of 1693.[10] Jefferson wrote Quesada in 1791 thanking him for the change of policy. But Jefferson assumed that the Spanish would assist Georgia residents in rounding up runaway slaves. He informed Quesada that Indian agent James Seagrove would negotiate with him for a return of the slaves. In 1791, George Washington wrote Seagrove to clarify his objective. Washington informed him of a confidential aspect of his mission: "Your first care will be to arrest the further reception of fugitive slaves, your next to obtain restitution of these slaves who have fled to Florida since the date of Governor Quesada's letter to Mr. Jefferson, notifying the orders of his Catholic Majesty. And your last object, which may demand the greatest address, will be to give a retrospective force to the orders of the Court of Spain, beyond the date of that letter, and to procure the Governor's order for a general relinquishment of all fugitive slaves, who were the property of the United States."[11]

Under the Continental Congress, Jay had demanded a repeal of the edict. The Congressional Committee on the State of Southern Indian Affairs demanded that the Creeks secure the return of all slaves, prisoners, and fugitives. Under the Washington administration, Jefferson had successfully completed the efforts begun by Jay to repeal the 1693 edict. Though the edict had been at the core of the Spanish defensive strategy, perhaps its relinquishment in the 1790s was a sign of the lessening of the Spanish desire to fight wars for Florida. In March 1791, Jefferson expressed optimism that Spain would help round up the various slaves. By May, Washington secretly pressed Seagrove to secure an order from Governor Quesada for the "general relinquishment" of fugitives.

Washington's letter to Seagrove was essentially the blueprint of U.S. strategy for confronting the Florida allies. He demanded payment to U.S. slaveholders for their losses in Florida and sought the repossession of all blacks claimed by U.S. citizens. The pursuit of Washington's objectives would follow the well-worn paths of first diplomacy, then war.

Washington and Jefferson had, in a very short time, used diplomacy to accomplish a goal that had eluded the British Parliament, the proprietors of South Carolina and Georgia, and their colonial administrators. Britain and the United States knew that historically the edict was at the core of Spain's strength in Florida. Washington and Jefferson, however, did not draw parallels between the end of the policy and the current weakness of Spain in Florida. During the years of British occupation, the power base of the blacks and Indians had shifted from St. Augustine to the Florida countryside, now the heartland of a new people, the Seminoles. Most likely, "Seminole country" was the primary destination of runaways from Georgia. To a great extent, the Seminoles came into being as a consequence of the edict's 100-year history. Spain could not have marched into the countryside and delivered the Seminoles to the United States. Therefore, though the Washington administration had eliminated the edict, it was also attempting to accomplish another goal that had eluded the British—the return of slaves.

The process of negotiating with Creeks and other natives for the capture of runaway slaves was begun by the British. Creeks had assisted the British to capture native and African slaves. Even before the Washington administration, the Continental Congress stipulated the return of African slaves in treaties with at least 13 tribes.[12] The Continental Congress had been negotiating with the Creeks for a treaty that would incorporate the return and apprehension of Georgia slaves. Finally, in 1790, Secretary of War Henry Knox negotiated a treaty with the Creeks. The Treaty of New York was specifically worded to include all the Creeks: Upper, Lower, and Seminole. Even a middle group of Creeks was mentioned. Article 3 of the treaty stated the following: "The Creek Nation shall deliver as soon as practical to the commanding officer of the troops of the United States, stationed at the Rock-Landing on the Oconee River, all citizens of the U.S., white inhabitants or Negroes, who are now prisoners in any part of the said nation. And if such prisoners or Negroes should not be so delivered, on or before the first day of June ensuing, the governor of Georgia may empower three persons to repair to the said nation, in order to claim and receive such prisoners and Negroes."[13]

There were some secret articles within the Treaty of New York. The Washington administration agreed to pay Creek Chief McGillivray $1,200 annually and to make him a brigadier general. Lesser chiefs were paid $100 annually.[14] The secret articles may have been unconstitutional. In *The Exiles of Florida*, Congressman Joshua Giddings of Ohio expresses the belief that Washington was secretly spending the nation's tax dollars in support of slave catching.[15] The public articles of the treaty clearly stated that the Creeks agreed to return runaway slaves. The secret articles do not specifically say that any payment is for the return of slaves. However, paying Creeks to catch slaves was a tradition that was more than a century old. Under the British the practice was not controversial; but for the United States, the issue of spending federal tax dollars to support slavery was potentially explosive.

Many objectives between the United States and the Creeks were stated in the treaty. Whether Washington intended to pay the Creeks to catch slaves or to pay them for some other purpose stated in the treaty, the result followed patterns set up during colonial days. The Creeks were expected to go to Florida and gather slaves. Instead of being paid by the British, they now were being paid by the United States to accomplish some technically unspecified objective.

By 1791, the Washington administration had established policies that were designed to respond to the problems of the Georgia slaveholders. Specifically, the administration hoped that the flow of slaves into Florida would cease and that the Spaniards in St. Augustine or the Creeks of Georgia and Florida would capture them.

In Congress, funding for Washington's treaties concerning natives was initially voted down, but James Madison maneuvered passage on a subsequent vote. The Georgia delegation assured Congress that war continued with the Creeks.[16] Though Washington and Jefferson were using diplomacy to address the problems in Florida, it seems that they ultimately planned to gain possession of Florida. In 1791, a few months after negotiations were completed with the Creeks and the Spanish, Jefferson notified Washington that Governor Quesada had issued a new order that allowed U.S. citizens to settle in Florida with their slaves. Jefferson believed that the Spanish hoped to weaken the border states by luring debtors. In spite of the Spanish ploy, he believed that the United States could eventually fill Florida with enough Americans to annex it without a war. Shortly afterward, Jefferson received a letter from a U.S. diplomat in Paris, William Short. Short told Jefferson that the Marquis de Lafayette had said that if the United States annexed Florida, the French would not fight a war in support of its Spanish ally.[17]

Jefferson's correspondence implies at least that the United States was considering a military response to the activities on the Florida-Georgia border. His letter to Washington perhaps weighs a covert response rather than an overt action. It is possible that the Washington administration was sounding out the French response to a war to annex Florida. During a congressional recess in 1791, Jefferson wrote to Madison directly addressing the issue: "Spain is unquestionably picking [a] quarrel with us.... The inevitableness of war with the Creeks, and the probability... of it with Spain (for there is not one of us who doubts it) will certainly occasion your convocation. At what time I cannot exactly say. But you should be prepared for this important change in the state of things."[18]

Most likely, Jefferson was informing Madison that if the Seminoles invaded Georgia, Congress would have to be brought back to consider war. The following year, Washington warned the Senate of trouble on the border with Spain that could lead to war. Senator James Jackson of Georgia introduced a bill that authorized defense expenditures if the state were invaded during recess.[19]

In spite of treaties between the United States and the Creeks and the elimination of the Spanish edict, border troubles persisted. The political situation for the Washington administration was in many ways similar to that during colonial days. If Parliament had been able to convince Spain to revoke the Edict of 1693, perhaps colonial development would have proceeded, costly wars would have been avoided, and debates over defense expenditures would have been unnecessary. The United States had succeeded in revoking the edict, but in the interim, between 1763 and 1783, a strong and relatively autonomous Seminole people had emerged. The Seminoles were not really consulted about Washington's two-track strategy for solving the political crisis on the Georgia-Florida border.

In all probability, it was in the interests of a weaker Spain to concede to U.S. demands on the edict. Washington had made generous concessions to the Creek chiefs. One Seminole chief was even present at the signing of the Treaty of New York. In general, though, the interests of the Seminoles were not considered. By the 1790s, it was highly probable that a disproportionate percentage of the Seminole military strength was African. Washington was prepared to negotiate with Indians among the Seminoles, but to Africans he offered only slavery. During colonial days, the British-Creek agreements directed Creeks to go to Florida and capture Apalachees for the slave industry; but by now there may have been 600 to 1,000 Africans in Florida, who were allies of Native Seminoles.

It seems that George Washington himself realized that the large group of blacks, which was of such value as slaves, was the crux of the problem. During treaty negotiations with the Creeks, he gave instructions to the Indian commissioners to find out how many Seminoles were living among the Creek nation.[20] As Washington discussed the treaty with the Senate, he said, "I flatter myself that this treaty will be productive of present peace and prosperity to our southern frontier."[21] A few years after the treaty was signed, Washington informed the House and the Senate that it was impossible for the Creeks to comply, specifically with the part of the treaty that required the return of slaves.[22]

There appears to have been a lot of uncertainty concerning the identity of the people at war with Georgia. Parallels to the pre-1763 allies of St. Augustine were apparent. Jay, Washington, Jefferson, and Madison all acknowledged a relationship between the former Spanish offer of freedom to slaves, their escape from Georgia, and later attacks on the United States. Washington and Jefferson believed that this complex situation would lead to war, but they were unsure of whether most of the blame belonged with Spain or with the Lower Creeks. Nevertheless, neither man went so far as to blame the ex-slaves. Only third parties were blamed. Washington told the Senate that the Creeks could not return the slaves. He and Jefferson had once believed that the African slaves resided among the Lower Creeks or Seminoles, and they assumed that turning them over to the United States would be only a formality.

References to the Seminoles began during the British occupation of Florida. By the time of the Washington administration, the nation seemed to be coming to an understanding about who the Seminoles were and what their exact role might have been in the border region. Even the congressmen from Georgia seemed uncertain of which natives to blame for their troubles.

The Treaties of San Lorenzo and New York, discussed below, underscore state and federal efforts to secure the slave industry. Washington instructed Indian agent Seagrove to make a special effort to obtain all slaves. Early in the administration, Jefferson and Washington discussed affidavits from residents along the Florida-Georgia border about the parties of blacks and natives who invaded and took slaves while spreading havoc. Now, Washington had to admit to Congress that his apprehension about the treaties with Creeks had been justified; they could not get any slaves.[23]

In 1794, Washington again told Congress that the treaty with the Creeks was not effective and that the nation was closer to war with Spain. The same year, Congressman Thomas Carnes of Georgia requested an end to the policy of giving presents to the Creek chiefs, because they were not executing their part of the treaty. Washington and Carnes exhibited new documentation that the Creeks had continued the practice of attacking Georgia.[24] The statements of Washington and Carnes are ambiguous. It is unclear whether they were referring to Seminoles, Lower Creeks, or Upper Creeks. In all probability, it is the Seminoles and the Lower Creeks who continued to attack, while the Upper Creeks were unable to fulfill their promise to return the Black Seminoles to slavery.

In 1795, the Washington administration negotiated the Treaty of San Lorenzo with Spain. This treaty formalized the end of Spanish edicts that advertised freedom for U.S.-owned slaves. Spain agreed to return all slaves among the Seminoles to their U.S. masters and to prevent the Seminoles from attacking the U.S. frontier. The Treaty of San Lorenzo overlapped the provisions of the Treaty of New York. The former gave Spain and the Upper Creeks the responsibility for subduing the Seminoles and capturing the rebels.[25]

By this time, it seems that in the words and actions of Washington and Jefferson, we can see the genesis of U.S. policy to obtain Spanish Florida. Neither the diplomatic negotiations with Spain in the wake of the revocation of the edict nor the objectives stated in the Treaties of New York and San Lorenzo had yielded success for the nation. As long as the institution of slavery was threatened in Georgia, the governor and representatives would continue to demand war. The administration's acknowledged failure meant not only that the Georgia frontier was ravaged, but also that political pressure continued from the state. The failure of the administration's policy also meant that Georgians were not able to fully open their lands for development. Madison had already stated that, by attacking Georgia, Spain hoped to prevent settlers from getting too close to Florida. This fact alone provided ample grounds for complaining to the administration. But additional debates arose in Congress over Georgia's defense expenditures. Georgia's congressional representatives spearheaded the battle for its citizens.

In the Fifth Congress, 1796–97, Congressman John Milledge of Georgia said that the House knew that the state was under fire, and he demanded that a provisional army be created to protect the state. Abraham Baldwin of Georgia pointed out that, in 1785, Georgia had signed a treaty with the Creeks in which extensive territory was given to the state. However, in the treaty negotiations of 1790, the administration gave the land back to the Creeks. Baldwin attributed this action simply to Creek hostilities.[26]

Even greater debates arose over Georgia's claims for general defense expenditures against the attacks from Creeks, most likely Seminoles. On this issue the Speaker of the House of Representatives during the Second Congress presented correspondence between the governor of Georgia and Secretary of War Henry Knox. This correspondence covered the years 1792–95 and showed that Knox authorized Georgia to incur militia expenses for self-defense. In addition, the governor of Georgia claimed that Knox had authorized assistance from South Carolina, too. Certain members of Congress argued that the Georgians exceeded Knox's allowances. The Georgians demanded full payments for lands given to the Creeks and for militia expenses.[27]

Compared to British colonial expenses in Georgia and Carolina, Georgia's expenditures were very predictable. In fact, the entire political strategy of the Washington administration closely paralleled the British experience. Georgia's demands on Congress for defense expenditures were preceded by colonial South Carolina's request to Parliament after the Yamasee War, as well as Oglethorpe's consistent demands. The British colonial politicians had been resolved to settle on a simple solution: Because Spanish attacks limited colonial expansion, the British had to take St. Augustine by force. Parliament, the colonial leaders, and Oglethorpe all agreed. War, however, did not solve the problems; the peace treaty of 1763 did.

During the Washington administration, the genesis of this same solution was evident. Washington's and Jefferson's acknowledgment that the United States must obtain Florida was implicit. Though there was ambiguity about whom to blame for policy failures, ultimately, the administration seemed to blame Spain. Washington and Jefferson therefore believed that war with Spain was inevitable, if not imminent. Washington stated this to both houses of Congress. Jefferson discussed it with Madison, and he notified Washington that Spain's strongest ally, France, would not interfere if the United States seized

Florida by force. But Jefferson also notified Washington of a peaceful strategy to obtain Florida. He discussed with Washington covert measures to be achieved through Spain's willingness to allow American settlers.

Therefore, in observing the Washington administration's policies and responses, we can see the genesis of the U.S. goal not only to settle disputes, but also to obtain Florida, by war or peace. The British had opted for war. Washington set the United States on the path to get Florida by either means. During the days of colonial Georgia and South Carolina, various politicians, including James Oglethorpe, expressed the belief that Florida threatened the existence of British colonialism in the Southeast and that either the Spanish would take Georgia and South Carolina, or the British must take Florida. By the time of the Jefferson administration, the acquisition of Florida by either war or peace was a dominant issue.[28]

In *The History of the United States of America*, Henry Adams wrote:

> During the administrations of Jefferson and Madison, the national government was in the main controlled by ideas and interests peculiar to the region south of the Potomac, and only to be understood from a Southern standpoint. Especially its foreign relations were guided by motives in which the Northern people felt little sympathy. . . . Among the varied forms of Southern ambition, none was so constant in influence as the wish to acquire the Floridas . . . yet the Northern public, though complaining of Southern favoritism, neither understood nor cared to study the subject . . . as if this were a local detail which in no way concerned the North. If Florida failed to interest the North, it exercised the more control over the South, and over a government Southern in character and purpose. Neither the politics of the union nor the development of events could be understood without treating Florida as a subject of first importance.[29]

Adams observed that Jefferson's "overmastering passion" was to buy or take Florida by force.[30] In the above comments, Adams also shows that the issue of Florida was more relevant to the South than to the North. Implicit in his comments is the conclusion that the southern obsession with Florida primarily emphasized legitimate competition between the United States, France, and Britain. Jefferson sought to include all Spanish territory along the Gulf of Mexico and east of the Mississippi in the Louisiana Purchase. The territory was known as East and West Florida. The British did not want to see East Florida granted to the United States. Adams seems to place these foreign policy considerations as paramount justification for the U.S. obsession.[31]

In "Jefferson and an American Foreign Policy," Walter LaFeber attributes Jefferson's outlook on Florida to the goal of expanding the boundaries of the United States by the conquest or purchase of Florida. However, he does comment on the problem of limited interference by the Spanish government. It seems that LaFeber's key concern was that imperial Spain was growing ever weaker. Consequently, the Spanish did not have sufficient power in the region to prevent clashes between the Seminoles and the white settlers pushing southward from Georgia.[32] LaFeber does not mention the presence of runaway slaves in the border clashes between "Indians and settlers." But his reasoning does demonstrate Seminole interference with the economic development of Georgia.

According to D. W. Meinig's *The Shaping of America*, the Jefferson administration wanted to keep Florida from falling into the hands of France or Britain. Meinig believes that the national policy under Jefferson was that Florida should and would, by one way or another, become an American territory. Having stated the general apprehension with the French or British goals, Meinig asserts that the primary drive to acquire Florida came from slaveholders of Georgia, Tennessee, and other nearby states. Meinig writes of the official rationale of southern leaders: Southern political and economic leaders viewed Florida with fear and apprehension. Its very existence ran counter to the goals of their policymakers. Its black militias and villages were proof that Florida was a world beyond the jurisdiction of both Spain and the United States.[33]

Though it is apparent that the United States had legitimate fears of Florida's somehow being transferred to Britain or France, Adams, LaFeber, and Meinig underscore what appear to have been the primary concerns: The southerners' proximity to Florida, dependence on the slave industry, and long legacy of fighting Florida guerrillas were more ominous than any possible threat from Europe. Jefferson continued to seek the annexation of East and West Florida by diplomacy, but it was impossible for the French to include the Floridas with the Louisiana Purchase.[34]

The U.S. justification for obtaining Florida was an ancient colonial legacy, but perhaps the excuse of seeking to block the French and the British provided a vague diplomatic cover. The colonial legacy was essentially southern. If blocking the British and French had been critical to U.S. interests, then Adams may have been able to count the northerners among those Americans obsessed with Florida. In 1803, Senator Jackson of Georgia discussed Florida: "Whom, then, should we have to contend with? With the bayonets of the intrepid French grenadiers... or with the enervated, degraded, and emaciated Spaniards? Shall we be told that we are no match for these emaciated beings?... I again repeat, sir, that I do not believe that Spain will venture war with the United States. I believe that she dare not; if she does, she will pay the cost. The Floridas will be immediately ours; they will almost take themselves."[35]

Senator Jackson's comments to the Senate were representative of the southern perspective on the need to acquire Florida, which occurred during Jefferson's diplomatic efforts surrounding the Louisiana Purchase. Jefferson, who had discussed covert measures for acquiring Florida, advised Washington in 1791 that it was possible to overwhelm Florida with such a large number of American settlers that the United States could acquire it without war. In the general scheme of getting Florida by any means, a variant of Jefferson's concept was executed during the Madison administration.

On 17 October 1810, John Rhea presided over a convention of U.S. citizens living in West Florida, near New Orleans. Led by Rhea, this convention of U.S. citizens requested that West Florida be annexed to the United States. Madison then authorized the governor of Louisiana to occupy West Florida by 27 October 1810. A number of these U.S. citizens then sparked a small rebellion against the Spanish government in the region. By December, Florida's Governor Juan Folch notified Havana that he must capitulate because of the presence of the Americans, unless military aid was sent.[36]

Though a French diplomat accused Madison of using the "rebellious association of a band of desperados" for the purpose of "wrestling a province from a friendly power," the secret U.S. effort to possess all of Florida was in progress.[37]

At the beginning of the third session of the 11th Congress, 3 January 1811, Madison called both houses together in a secret session. He notified Congress that he had received a letter of capitulation from Governor Folch of Florida. Madison then asked for authority and expenditures to annex both East and West Florida to prevent British occupation. Madison reminded Congress of the unending conflict along the Georgia-Florida border. According to Madison, "[T]aking into view...the intimate relation of the country adjoining the United States, eastward of the river Perdido (near Pensacola), to their security and tranquillity, and the peculiar interest they otherwise have in its destiny," the action was essential.[38]

On 15 January 1811, after 30 votes, Congress passed a bill in secret session that granted Madison the authority to use military force or diplomacy to obtain Florida.[39] Madison gave secret orders to former Georgia Governor George Mathews to execute the mission of seizing East Florida. Madison directed Mathews to assemble a force that could prompt a scenario similar to what had happened in West Florida. Americans already living in East Florida were urged to declare themselves sovereign and then request annexation to the United States. Mathews's job was to facilitate the effort. But to ensure a sufficient pretext for seizing Florida, Madison told Mathews to immediately seize the territory if he suspected an impending British action.[40]

In 1812, Mathews's expedition got under way. In *The Seminole*, Edwin C. McReynolds wrote, "Early in 1812, General Mathews planned an uprising in East Florida, which he hoped would have the appearance of a spontaneous revolt."[41] Mathews encountered unexpected trouble when a U.S. commander refused to furnish him with gunboats in southern Georgia. It seems that the commander was unaware of Mathews's expedition and that information about the secret plan had leaked to the wrong sources, causing some embarrassment to the administration. To disguise the overall plan, Mathews was dismissed and accused of not following orders. By April, Georgia Governor David Mitchell was put in charge. As with Mathews, his instructions from Secretary of State Monroe were ambiguous. Monroe essentially ordered Mitchell to discover the best diplomatic pretext for acquiring Florida with the help of the American rebels.[42]

By May 1813, it was apparent that Madison's attempt to acquire East Florida by both diplomatic and military efforts was a total failure. Congress therefore forced a withdrawal of U.S. troops. During the two-and-a-half-year effort, though, the true nature of the American struggle in Florida had become more evident. In December 1812, Congress requested all facts relating to the Florida effort. Madison sent a secret report to Congress that contained correspondence from various officials. In the report, the leader of the American rebels, John McIntosh, complained about overall U.S. support.

Our slaves incited to rebel, and we have an army of Negroes raked up in this country and brought from Cuba to contend with. Let us ask, if we are abandoned, what will be the situation of the southern states with this body of men in the neighborhood? St. Augustine the whole province, will be the refuge of fugitive slaves; and from thence emissaries can, and no doubt will, be detached, to bring about a revolt of the Black population in the United States. A nation that can stir up the savages round your western frontiers to murder, will hesitate but little to introduce the horrors of St. Domingo into your southern country.[43]

In this letter, McIntosh made clear that he believed he should get more federal support. Though many congressmen believed that the primary source of opposition was the Spanish, there may also have been a considerable degree of opposition from the Black Seminoles. In *The Plot to Steal Florida*, Joseph B. Smith reaches a similar conclusion. Smith comments on the U.S. troops' occupation of the ruins of Fort Mose. According to Smith: "They were taking possession of a place that was a symbol of what their operation was finally to become, a racial conflict. . . . When James Oglethorpe invaded Florida . . . a major battle took place at Moosa on June 15, 1740. A force of three hundred blacks and Indians nearly wiped out his army."[44]

Though Spain reinforced St. Augustine with black Cuban forces, it appears that the Black and Native Seminoles were the principle opponents of the United States. Before initiating the attack on Florida, Mathews had sat down with the Seminole chief, Payne, and had convinced him to remain neutral; however, while these negotiations were in progress, a black envoy arrived from St. Augustine and convinced the Seminoles to assist the Spanish. The leaders of the Upper Creeks also tried to convince the Seminoles to stay neutral or, they said, all Creeks would lose their land.[45]

In June 1812, the new Spanish governor, Sebastian Kindelan, sent a letter to Governor Mitchell: "A number of seditious persons, who were disturbing the peace of the country, occupied and fortified a house on Moosa from whence they could overlook the operations of this place. . . . The constant sight and proximity of them were very insulting to the loyal inhabitants of this city. . . . My predecessor decided on sending a small party to dislodge the rebels as was done."[46]

Mitchell responded indignantly to Kindelan. He chastised the Spaniards for fighting back with black troops and said that the Spanish actions at Mose were unjustified. Mitchell complained, "There is however another subject which the candor that characterizes the United

States government requires me to present to your consideration; I mean the Black troops which you have in your service. Your certain knowledge of the peculiar situation of the southern section of the Union, in regard to that description of people, one might have supposed would have induced you to abstain from introducing them into the province."[47]

Mitchell's response to Kindelan is very ironic. He had just invaded Florida. Fort Mose was the most strategic location for invading St. Augustine. It was only logical for the Spanish to attack. But Mitchell's position on black troops reflects the southern obsession with Florida that Adams points out. It seems that the South placed the institution of slavery above all else. In dislodging the Americans from Fort Mose, Spain used a force of Spanish, blacks, and Indians from St. Augustine. Mitchell estimated that there were 500 black and 400 white soldiers there. But these statistics are questionable when one considers other statements made by Mitchell.

In a letter to Secretary of State James Monroe, Mitchell comments on the actions of Florida Governor Kindelan: "The same governor has proclaimed freedom to every Negro who will join his standard and has sent a party of them to unite with, and who are actually at this time united with the Indians in their murderous excursions. Indeed the principle strength of the garrison of St. Augustine consists of Negroes, there being but a few militia of the province in the place who adhered to the royal government when the revolution broke out, . . . [a]n old battalion of regular troops whom it is understood would surrender without firing a shot."[48]

If 900 soldiers were in St. Augustine, Mitchell could not have expected such an easy surrender. Though they were expelled from Fort Mose, U.S. forces had St. Augustine under siege for 5 months and on the verge of starvation. At this point, the Spanish sent an envoy to the Seminoles for help, which brought a force of 200 to 300 Black and Native Seminoles into the struggle. Coming from their towns in the forest, the Seminoles launched guerrilla raids on those U.S. forces that surrounded St. Augustine. They also raided the settlements of Americans living in Florida, many of whom were among those forces laying siege to St. Augustine.

This two-phased attack broke the siege. Governor Mitchell notified Monroe that Kindelan had armed every able-bodied black man in the province and that he, Mitchell, had sent for reinforcements. From Georgia, Major Daniel Newnan arrived with 250 volunteers in August.

The Seminoles used the same strategy. They launched guerrilla raids on Newnan while sparking slave revolts and raiding plantations in Georgia. Many Georgia volunteers fled home to safeguard their families, homes, and slaves. Many of the U.S. patriots and rebels who had originally started with Mathews in Florida abandoned their plantations and fled north.[49]

The siege of St. Augustine was led by Colonel Thomas Smith, who reported to Governor Mitchell that his men were sick with fever from the rains and that the environment was very unhealthy. He noted that 105 of his 270 men were at all times on the sick list. He said that his forces were hit 20 miles north of St. Augustine by a "motley set of Red and Black savages," 40 to 50 in number. Smith reported that the Seminoles were led by a black man named Prince. Though the Seminoles killed all of the horses on a U.S. wagon train, many Americans escaped. Smith told Mitchell that he could not attack St. Augustine without 300 to 400 more men. Mitchell told Monroe in October that if troops were withdrawn, Georgia would be attacked and that only the entire military strength of the state could save her. While war raged in Florida, Mitchell informed Monroe that "[m]ost of our male Negroes are restless on the seaboard . . . and attempt to get to Augustine. . . . Many have succeeded, . . . which renders it necessary to have constant guards and patrols."[50]

In spite of Mitchell's fears, Colonel Smith was convinced by the attack on his wagon train to evacuate his forces to Georgia. He had help from Major Newnan's forces. With the siege of St. Augustine lifted and a continuous flow of alarming correspondence arriving from the frontier, any hope of seizing East Florida may have been lost by August. By this time, it was perhaps clear that the primary U.S. battlefield enemy was the Seminoles.

In September, Major Newnan was sent on a search-and-destroy mission against the Seminole villages. Newnan had 116 men, many of them sick with malaria. Before reaching any Seminole villages, Newnan's troops were ambushed by a force of 75 to 100 Seminoles. The U.S. forces were kept at bay without food for a week; however, the Americans had far superior weapons. Finally, the Seminoles allowed them to make a night escape. Even though they had successfully evaded severe casualties, Newnan's forces were hit by guerrilla attacks as they retreated back into Georgia. On arrival in Georgia, Newnan remarked that "Negroes are the best soldiers."[51]

With Newnan's failure, Mitchell notified Monroe, "Sir, the affairs of East Florida have assumed, within a few weeks past, a very serious and alarming aspect." He told Monroe, "[T]he Seminole within the Florida line are determined upon war with us." Mitchell believed that the Seminoles were inspired by the Spanish, but he thought that if a war with them was necessary, it was better to chase them into Florida and destroy their towns.[52]

Between February and May 1813, Colonel Smith led 400 men into Seminole country on a search-and-destroy mission. The Seminoles were outnumbered 2 to 1 on the battlefield. Therefore, they hid their women and children in the swamps. Smith succeeded in destroying two Seminole towns and confiscated 2,000 deerskins and 1,000 head of cattle. Though Smith succeeded in destroying the towns, the Seminoles continued to wage a guerrilla campaign. Their persistence convinced Congress to order U.S. forces out of Florida in May 1813.[53]

The unsuccessful effort by the Madison administration to get Florida was the culmination of efforts begun by the Continental Congress. The United States, like Britain before it, had to first surmount the diplomatic hurdles before it could seek a military solution. The Continental Congress had inherited an unsolved problem with extensive political implications from the British. The records show that while Florida was British territory, between 1763 and 1783, depredations along the Florida-Georgia frontier, though diminished, continued as during the Spanish era. In the wake of the American Revolution, the Continental Congress nonetheless fixed the primary blame for the border problems on Spain. As secretary of state for the Continental Congress, John Jay alerted Madison, Washington, and Jefferson to the complaints of their fellow southerners. Even during the colonial days, the problem of fighting Florida was, to a degree, a sectional issue. Northern colonies had little interest in the faraway needs of South Carolina and Georgia. However, in Parliament the issue had greater general relevance.

After the Spanish reestablished themselves in Florida, the Continental Congress initiated a diplomatic strategy for solving the complaints of the state of Georgia. First, efforts were made to end the Spanish policy of freeing all slaves who escaped into Florida, and second, Congress initiated treaties with the Creeks for the return of slaves. The diplomatic efforts with Spain were a colonial legacy, but the Indian diplomacy reflects the rise of a consolidated Seminole people. Though the treaty negotiations essentially excluded the Seminoles, by the 1780s, the United States was aware of the existence of an autonomous group of Indians who could wage war and facilitate freedom for runaway slaves. Some Seminoles were Lower Creeks, but it appears likely that early diplomats did not understand the true political distinction between the Seminoles, the Upper Creeks, and the Lower Creeks.

Notes

1. Benjamin Quarles, *The Negro in the American Revolution* (New York, London: W. W. Norton and Co., 1961), 118, 126, 151.

2. Chapter 2 gives a detailed explanation of the creation of the Seminole people.

3. Fitzpatrick, ed., *Journals of the Continental Congress*, vol. 28, 1774–1789, 118, vol. 34, 326, 430–31.

4. Ibid., vol. 28, 119.

5. Ibid., vol. 34, 326.

6. Ibid., 327.

7. Ibid., 430–31; Jay, *Correspondence*, 259, 357.

8. James Madison, *The Papers of James Madison*, vol. 10, 1787–1788, ed. Robert A. Rutland (Chicago: University of Chicago Press, 1962), 219.

9. Thomas Jefferson, *The Papers of Thomas Jefferson*, vol. 16, ed. Julian P. Boyd (Princeton, N.J.: Princeton University Press, 1961), 329, 450; vol. 17, 472.

10. Ibid., vol. 17, 638.

11. George Washington, *The Writings of George Washington*, vol. 31, 1745–1799, ed. John C. Fitzpatrick (Washington, D.C.: U.S. Government Printing Office, 1939), 288–90.

12. Kappler, *Indian Affairs*, 4–8, 14, 16.

13. Ibid., 26.

14. Miller, *Treaties*, vol. 2, 344.

15. Giddings, *Exiles*, chap. 1.

16. *Annals of Congress*, vol. 2, 1st Cong., 1st sess., 8 August 1789, 724–30.

17. Jefferson, *Papers*, vol. 20, 97, 530.

18. Madison, *Papers*, vol. 15, 37.

19. *Annals of Congress*, 3d Cong., 2d sess., 20 May 1794, 102.

20. George Washington, *The Papers of George Washington*, Presidential Series, vol. 4, ed. W. W. Abbot and Dorothy Twohig (Charlottesville, Va., and London: University Press of Virginia, 1993), 559.

21. *Am. St. P.*, 2, *Indian Affairs*, 1:81.

22. Ibid., 546.

23. Ibid.

24. *Annals of Congress*, vol. 1, 3d Cong., 1st sess., 20 May 1794, 102, 117, 1170.

25. Miller, *Treaties*, vol. 2, 318–23.

26. *Annals of Congress*, vol. 2, 5th Cong., 2d sess., 5 January 1800, 1949; *Annals of Congress*, vol. 3, 5th Cong., 3d sess., 10 October 1800, 2547; *Annals of Congress*, 7th Cong., 2d sess., 7 January 1804, 461.

27. *Annals of Congress*, 7th Cong., 2d sess., 7 January 1804, 461.

28. Henry Adams, *History of the United States of America*, vol. 2, *During the First Administration of Thomas Jefferson* (New York: Charles Scribner's Sons, 1921), 245–46.

29. Henry Adams, *History of the United States of America*, vol. 1, *During the Administration of Jefferson and Madison* (Englewood Cliffs, N.J.: Prentice-Hall, 1963), 113.

30. Adams, *History of the United States: Jefferson and Madison*, vol. 2, 245.

31. Henry Adams, *History of the United States, 1801–1809* (New York: Literary Classics of the United States, 1986), 271–79.

32. Walter LaFeber, "Jefferson and an American Foreign Policy," in *Jeffersonian Legacies*, ed. Peter Onuf (Charlottesville, Va.: University Press of Virginia, 1993), 382.

33. D. W. Meinig, *The Shaping of America*, vol. 2 (New Haven, Conn.: Yale University Press, 1993), 26–31.

34. *Annals of Congress*, 7th Cong., 2d sess., March–April 1804, 1011, 1014, 1020, 1183.

35. *Annals of Congress*, vol. 1, 8th Cong., 1st sess., 12 January 1805, 39.

36. *Annals of Congress*, 11th Cong., 3d sess., October 1810–January 1811, 1251–59; Smith, Plot, 107.

37. *Annals of Congress*, 11th Cong., 3d sess., 15 December 1810, 1261.

38. Ibid., 3 January 1811, 369, 370; Smith, *Plot*, 112.

39. *Annals of Congress*, 11th Cong., 3d sess., 15 January 1811, 377.

40. *Annals of Congress*, vol. 2, 12th Cong., 3d sess., 26 January 1811, 1687.

41. Edwin C. McReynolds, *The Seminoles* (Norman, Okla.: University of Oklahoma Press, 1957), 44.

42. *Annals of Congress*, vol. 2, 12th Cong., 1st sess., 4 April–27 May 1812, 1689–92; *State Papers and Publick Documents of the United States*, Series 1, vol. 9, 3d ed. (Boston: Thomas B. Wait, 1819), 161–62.

43. *State Papers*, 156.

44. Smith, *Plot*, 211.

45. *State Papers*, 181–84.

46. Ibid., 193.

47. Ibid., 195; Kenneth W. Porter, *The Negro on the American Frontier* (New York: Arno Press and the New York Times, 1971), 192.

48. *State Papers*, 169, 174, 178.

49. Ibid., 164–65; Porter, *Negro*, 192–94.

50. Porter, Negro, 194; *State Papers*, 170–76.

51. Porter, *Negro*, 195–98.

52. *State Papers*, 174–78.

53. Porter, *Negro*, 199–201; Mulroy, *Border*, 12; Covington, *Seminoles of Florida*, 28–29; Monroe, *Writings*, vol. 5, 1807–1816, 252.

Chapter 6

The First Seminole War, 1817–18*

In the years after the Patriots War, U.S. political and military leaders began to target the Black Seminoles in particular for destruction. The Black Seminoles were the logical target because MLR was the key threat to the southern economy. Previous efforts to placate the demands of the slave industry had prompted Washington and Jefferson to target Spain and the Creeks as the vehicle for solving the crisis with runaway slaves. This was made explicit in the initiatives to end the edict of 1693 and in the treaties at New York and San Lorenzo. The Patriots War further targeted Spain.

However, in 1816, U.S. policymakers once again decided to invade Florida, this time to destroy the "Negro fort" (see below). This action sparked the First Seminole War. In conducting this war, the United States seemed to target the Black Seminoles. The Washington Treaty of 1819 ceded Florida to the United States, as a quid pro quo for Spain's inability to honor the Treaty of San Lorenzo, which required the capture and return of rebels. In the 1821 Treaty of Indian Springs, the Upper Creek allies of the United States were forced to pay Georgians an indemnity of land and money for uncaptured Black Seminoles in Florida; additionally, under President James Monroe and Secretary of War John C. Calhoun, the U.S. government became the legal owners of

---

* See figure C on page 74.

the Black Seminoles. Therefore, although U.S. authorities knew they confronted an allied force of Africans and natives, the war and policies indicate that they now realized that the rebels represented the key opposition to the United States in Florida.

In 1819, Pennsylvania Senator Abner Lacock of the Senate Select Committee on the Seminole War issued a report. Lacock reported that the war was initiated by Upper Creeks who were dissatisfied with an 1814 treaty that confiscated their land. The report states that those Creeks were spurred on by two British agents, Robert Ambrister and Alexander Arbuthnot. Further, it states that the Creeks had launched numerous attacks on settlers and that U.S. General Edmund Gaines sought to apprehend them. Lacock says that the real war began when Lieutenant Robert Scott and about 40 other U.S. soldiers were massacred while serving under General Gaines. Lacock does not mention the "Negro fort" as a cause of hostilities.[1] In *The Seminoles of Florida*, James Covington cites another battle before Scott's massacre as the spark that ignited the war. He says Major David Twiggs and 250 soldiers attacked a Seminole village and killed four men and one woman. Covington mentions the U.S. attack on the fort, but he does not connect it directly to the First Seminole War.[2]

In *Freedom on the Border*, Kevin Mulroy describes the destruction of the fort. Though he does not suggest that the fort's destruction began the war, he shows continuous raids by the Seminoles as a direct response to it. Mulroy says that the First Seminole War began when Africans and natives united to oppose southern slave-catching expeditions. He does not mention Lieutenant Scott's massacre.[3]

Though neither Covington, Mulroy, nor Lacock's Senate select committee report attributes the war to being a consequence of the fort's destruction, all seem to show a series of responses and counterresponses that preceded the war. The First Seminole War could be traced back to the Patriots War, but it seems that the U.S. decision to destroy the fort marked the beginning of an effort to circumscribe the activities of the Black Seminoles.

The Negro Fort

The Negro fort originated in the War of 1812. British Colonel Edward Nicholls attempted to rally disaffected inhabitants of Louisiana, including slaves and natives, to the British cause. He issued a proclamation inviting all to join him. Perhaps as many as 100 Louisiana slaves accepted his offer. After British losses in Louisiana, Nicholls sailed into the Apalachee Bay of Florida, where again he sought allies among Africans and natives, this time the Seminoles. Nicholls promised the Native Seminoles that he would help them regain the land stolen by the United States, and he promised some of the Black Seminoles that he would resettle them as free citizens of Jamaica, Bermuda, or the Bahamas. Though the British government denounced Nicholls's behavior, it seems probable that he acted in the name of the government. With the help of the Seminoles and other allies, Nicholls built what became known as "the Negro fort." The fort was located 15 miles north of the mouth of the Apalachicola River on the east bank.[4] In February 1815, after the War of 1812 had ended, Nicholls abandoned the fort and left it in the possession of the Black Seminoles. Estimates of the fort's troop strength range from 250 to 450 Africans, plus a few dozen Indians.[5]

In a letter to the secretary of the Navy, Commodore Daniel Patterson wrote about the fort: "It had become the general rendezvous for runaway slaves and disaffected Indians. . . . The force of the Negroes was daily increasing; and they felt themselves so strong and secure that they had commenced several plantations on the fertile banks of the Apalachicola."[6] It seems that the combination of security and food made the fort and the vicinity a prime destination for runaway slaves. In *The Florida Wars*, Virginia B. Peters says that as many as 1,000 blacks lived near the fort.[7] Joshua Giddings reported that the blacks had 50 miles of plantations along the river, with their cattle and horses roaming wild in the forest.[8]

Probably nothing quite as ominous to the interests of the U.S. slave industry had ever existed. The fort was erected by Nicholls to support British interests, but the Black Seminoles and recent runaways could see that it served their goals. The Negro fort, to some degree, facilitated the phenomenon of macro-rebellion; but perhaps, ultimately, it worked against it. The problem of slaves fleeing to and thriving in Florida had been addressed diplomatically by George Washington's administration. Their actions caused Spain to revoke the 1693 edict, and in its place, they negotiated the 1790 Treaty of New York and the 1795 Treaty of San Lorenzo. These diplomatic efforts made third parties, Spain and the Upper Creeks, responsible for the behavior and ultimate capture and return of U.S.-claimed property (i.e., slaves). The late Patriots War had blatantly alerted Americans to the military skills of the Africans seeking to remain free or, at least, to preserve their Spanish ally. But in this war the Black Seminoles were still more of an appendage to the third parties.

To the extent that macro-rebellion was best facilitated by obscurity and indirect confrontation, the Negro fort would prove to be much too conspicuous. With very few natives in the region and its location far from the jurisdiction of any Spanish authority, the fort became an obvious target. Except for Nicholls, who had fled to London, there was no third party to focus U.S. attention on. Military and political policies now had to focus on the Black Seminoles almost exclusively. The United States offered no diplomatic courtesy to the rebellious Africans.

In May 1815, General Gaines notified the acting Secretary of War, A. J. Dallas, of the fort's existence. During the next year, there would be extensive correspondence between the War Department, General Gaines, and the U.S. commander of the Division of the South, General Andrew Jackson.[9]

In April 1816, General Jackson directed the following ultimatum to the Florida governor:

> I am charged by my Government to make known to you that a Negro fort, erected during our late war with Britain...is now occupied by upwards of two hundred and fifty Negroes, many of whom have been enticed from the service of their masters, citizens of the United States; all of whom are well-clothed and disciplined. Secret practices to inveigle Negroes from citizens of Georgia, as well as from the Cherokee and Creek nations of Indians, are still continued by this banditti and the hostile Creeks. This...may endanger the peace of the nation and interrupt the good understanding which so happily exists between our governments....
> The principles of good faith which always insure good neighborhood between nations, require the immediate and prompt interference of the Spanish authority to destroy or remove from our frontier this banditti, put an end to an evil of so serious a nature, and return to our citizens and friendly Indians inhabiting our territory those Negroes now in said fort....I reflect that the conduct of this banditti is such as will not be tolerated by our government, and if not put down by Spanish authority, will compel us, in self defense, to destroy them.[10]

Jackson was apparently expressing the policies of his immediate superior, the secretary of war. The United States reverted to diplomacy. Jackson gave a third party, the Spanish, one last opportunity to take responsibility for the actions of an apparently stateless people, the Black Seminoles. No longer was the rebels' status facilitated by others.

Now, the rebels were projected in a manner that the U.S. slave interests perceived as directly hostile and provocative. Jackson's effort to compel the Spanish to capture and return slaves reflects on the past failure of the previous administration.

Florida Governor Zuniga's response to Jackson also reflects on past Spanish policies. He informed Jackson that he was powerless to destroy the fort unless ordered to do so by the king of Spain. In addition, Zuniga told Jackson that the Spanish did not have enough military might in Florida to go against the blacks. Zuniga further clarified the American dilemma with the Black Seminoles:

> It gives me pleasure to understand that, thinking as your excellency thinks with respect to the necessity of destroying the Negroes, the fort at Apalachicola occupied by them was not constructed by orders of the Spanish government; and that the Negroes, although in part belonging to inhabitants of this province, and as rational beings, may be subjects of the King, my master, are deemed by me insurgents or rebels against the authority, not only of his Catholic Majesty, but also of the proprietors for whose service they have withdrawn themselves; some seduced by the English Colonel Nicholls, Major Woodbine, and their agents, and others from their inclination to run off.[11]

Here it appears that the macro-level rebellion (MLR) phenomenon had transcended the facilities of third parties. Before directly confronting the Black Seminoles in the fort, the United States seemed to make a final effort to allow Washington's diplomatic strategy to function. As the Treaty of San Lorenzo stipulated, Jackson demanded that the Spanish destroy the fort, capture the Africans, and return them to slavery. Zuniga's declaration of lacking orders from the king, seemed to be a return to the dilemma already solved by Jay, Washington, and Jefferson. However, his statement of Spain's apparent impotency in Florida was all too familiar to the Americans. Though the United States could have been seeking only those slaves recently removed by Nicholls from Louisiana during the war, Zuniga made it clear to Jackson that a wide variety of Africans were assembled in the region of the fort. Therefore, any U.S. effort to return slaves to their masters implicitly incorporated the provisions of treaties with Spain and the Creeks that specified that same objective.

Before the direct confrontation with the Black Seminoles, the United States attempted a diplomatic legacy of the Washington administration. In June 1816, General Jackson and Indian agent Hawkins ordered Creek allies to go to the fort, capture the Black Seminoles, and return them to their masters. But General Gaines told the secretary of war that this could not be achieved.[12]

Though not specifically stated as such, Jackson's orders to the Creeks and his ultimatum to the Florida governor were a final U.S. effort to enforce specific provisions of treaties signed by George Washington. With this final diplomatic effort proving just as unsuccessful, direct confrontation was imminent. That same month, Jackson notified Secretary of War William Crawford that "there can be no fear of disturbing the good understanding that exists between us and Spain, by destroying the Negro fort, and restoring to the owners the Negroes that may be captured."[13]

By July, Jackson ordered Colonel Clinch and Creek Chief McIntosh to go and destroy the Negro fort and return the slaves. A few Americans were killed in skirmishes with the Seminoles while holding the fort under siege. But on 27 July, a heated cannonball struck the powder magazine of the fort. A great explosion threw pieces of bodies high into the surrounding pine trees. Dead in the explosion were 270 men, women, and children. Approximately 334 rebels and 34 Native Seminoles were in the fort. These 34 natives were present because they had intermarried with the Africans. From the 60 survivors, Colonel Clinch selected one African and one native as symbolic chiefs of the fort. They were then tortured to death by the Creeks. The rest of the survivors were handed over to Georgia citizens, some who claimed to be descendants of original slave masters dating back to the colonial days.[14]

Previous U.S. incursions into Florida targeted either Spain or the Native Seminoles. This direct confrontation with the Black Seminole rebels now brought the nation face to face with the key issue of confrontation—the interests of the slave industry. The Negro fort threatened slavery, and its survivors were recycled into the industry. Perhaps also, for the first time in U.S. history, the objectives of the Washington administration were at least partially achieved. This partial success, however, was based on the use of U.S. troops as slave hunters. The destruction of the Negro fort can be seen as the beginning of the First Seminole War, or as the spark that initiated a chain of events that led to the war. Giddings wrote: "This commencement of the First Seminole War was ... undertaken for the purposes stated in General Jackson's order, to blow up the fort and return the Negroes to their rightful owners. Historians have failed to expose the cause of hostilities, or the barbarous foray which plunged the nation into that bloody contest which cost the people millions of treasure and the sacrifice of hundreds of human lives."[15]

Giddings's perspective underscores the viewpoint that the First Seminole War was indeed an effort of Americans to come to grips with a problem that had plagued the nation for years, one that had defied the efforts of presidents since Washington and the nation since the days of the Continental Congress. This perspective of Giddings's is underscored by John Quincy Adams in his memoirs as secretary of state: "A full exposition of the causes and origin of the war in Florida would be given in a dispatch to our minister in Spain, together with all the vouchers supporting the statements of facts; that the war would be traced to Nicholls and his Negro fort and that Arbuthnot will be shown to have been the cause of the renewal of the war."[16]

The statements of Giddings and Adams reflect on the event that initiated the war. Adams seems to suggest that the British agent Arbuthnot coaxed the Seminoles to continue hostilities. Such a perspective would suggest that the deaths of at least 270 men, women, and children would be less of a cause for war among the Black Seminoles.

By 1817, numerous reports were flooding into Washington of Seminole hostilities. U.S. citizens on the Georgia-Florida frontier were abandoning their farms and fleeing north or to forts. Cattle and hogs originally taken from U.S. plantations poured into Florida as confiscated possessions of the Seminoles. George Perryman reported to Lieutenant Richard Sands that Seminoles spoke of Americans with contempt and swore to get even for the destruction of the Negro fort. Other reports came in of hundreds of Black Seminole troops drilling in Florida. The major response to the destruction of the fort came in November 1817. The Seminole allies attacked a party of U.S. troops escorting women and children. This group was commanded by Lieutenant Scott. There were 40 soldiers, 7 women, and 4 children. Ironically, the attack occurred as Scott's party traveled up the Apalachicola River in a boat. Two soldiers escaped and one woman was taken prisoner. The rest were killed.[17]

In the months between the massacre at the Negro fort and the massacre of Lieutenant Scott's party, several confrontations occurred between Americans and Seminoles. None, though, were on such a significant scale. Previous attacks by the Seminoles could be interpreted as responses to the fort's destruction. However, the attack on Scott was the hostile event that prompted the U.S. escalation.

President James Monroe blamed Spain for the attack, insisting that the Spanish had failed to restrain the Seminoles as required by a 1795 treaty, and called the attack unwarranted. Secretary of War Calhoun ordered Generals Jackson and Gaines to pursue the Seminoles.[18] In December, before commencing full-scale attacks, Gaines notified Calhoun: "The Seminole Indians, however strange and absurd it may appear to those who understand little of their real character and extreme ignorance, entertain a notion that they cannot be beaten by our troops. They confidently assert that we have never beaten them. . . . They have little or no means of knowing the strength and resources of our country. . . . This error of theirs has led them from time to time, for many years past, to massacre our frontier citizens."[19]

It seems that General Gaines was not aware of the Seminole legacy. Perhaps the Seminoles referred to historical successes against attempts to re-enslave them going back to the 17th century. Gaines did not understand the Black Seminole will to resist slavery. It seems probable that this comment to Calhoun was, in particular, a reference to the blacks. Gaines informed the Seminole Chief Kenhagee, "You harbor a great many of my Black people among you at Suwanee. If you give me leave to go by you against them, I shall not hurt anything belonging to you."[20]

Gaines seemed, therefore, to believe that it was futile for the Black Seminoles to resist U.S. forces. His comments reflect a developing strategy to isolate the blacks. British traders or agents Alexander Arbuthnot and Robert Ambrister were charged by Jackson and Gaines with being accomplices of Colonel Nicholls's, selling weapons to Seminoles, and inciting the war. Both Arbuthnot and Ambrister were tried and executed by Andrew Jackson after the war. Before his death, Arbuthnot wrote a letter to his son:

> As I am ill able to write a long letter, it is necessary to be brief—under the immediate command of General Jackson, eighteen sail of vessels off Apalachicola. By a deserter that was brought here by the Indians, the commandant was informed that three thousand men, under the orders of General Jackson, one thousand foot and sixteen horse, under General Gaines, and five hundred under another General, were at Prospect Bluff [the Negro fort], where they are rebuilding the burnt fort; that one thousand Indians were at Spanish Bluff, building another fort under the direction of American officers; that so soon as their forts were built they intended to march. . . . The main drift of the Americans is to destroy the Black population of Suwanee. Tell my friend Boleck that it is just throwing away his people to attempt to resist such a powerful force. . . . So soon as the Suwanee is destroyed, I expect the Americans will be satisfied and retire; this is only my opinion; but I think it is conformable to the demand made by General Gaines of Kenhagee some months since.[21]

Arbuthnot reflects on the great odds that were clearly set against the Seminoles in general, but the Black Seminoles in particular. Some of his final thoughts in the midst of Jackson's invasion are further clues that suggest that the War Department was developing a strategy to eliminate the thriving Black Seminole towns. The existence of such a strategy was hardly perceptible and could not be openly discussed in Congress because of the delicacy of the slave issue.[22]

The Native Seminoles were the most numerous, but if they had been the primary adversary of the United States, Gaines would not have written Kenhagee. The Native Seminoles resided in a foreign country. If they had been raiding the U.S. frontier settlements and otherwise posing a consistent threat to the nation, it seems unlikely that Gaines would have sought to exempt them from punishment. However, if Gaines believed that both Black and Native Seminoles were guilty, then he showed a discretionary reaction to the activities of the blacks.

To the extent that Black Seminoles were the primary target of the U.S. troops, MLR in North America was at stake. Certainly, if the total Seminole military force was less than 1,000, then the blacks probably never exceeded 200 or 300. MLR was sustained by strategic guerrilla warfare. Therefore, to engage Jackson's formidable force was not in the best interests of any of the Seminoles. The adjutant general of the southern division of the U.S. Army reported to Congress that the Seminoles never put more than 500 men on the battlefield during the war.[23] The Seminole objective was merely to survive physically when attacked by Jackson's troops, but in some cases, their guerrilla tactics were useful. They had ambushed Lieutenant Scott's party on the Apalachicola. According to Major Peter Muhlenburg, at the beginning of the war they had used the same tactics to stop all U.S. supplies shipped on the Apalachicola.[24] In general, though, guerrilla tactics could not resist Jackson's two major campaigns of the war.

Jackson personally led the attacks. The first American assault came at Lake Miccosukee, about 10 miles south of the Georgia border or 20 miles northeast of present-day Tallahassee, Florida. Lake Miccosukee had several Black and Native Seminole villages with plantations and herds of cattle. Knowing of Jackson's approach, the blacks in particular moved their families far away and prepared to engage the U.S. forces. The Seminole forces divided into black and Indian regiments. As U.S. forces advanced, the Seminoles attacked from the most strategic sites possible; when U.S. reinforcements moved in, they fled in all directions to prevent pursuit. At Miccosukee the U.S. forces burned

300 homes and obtained 1,000 head of cattle for their troops, plus a large supply of corn.[25]

U.S. forces next captured the undefended Spanish fort at St. Marks, which is situated on the Apalachee Bay. Here the British trader Arbuthnot was apprehended. Just before his capture, Arbuthnot had sent the letter to Kenhagee warning of Jackson's approach. Leaving St. Marks, Jackson marched 10 miles southeast to attack the Seminole villages located on the Suwanee River, about 30 miles from its mouth. Here there was a black settlement of 400 people with plantations, herds of cattle and hogs, and well-built houses. As at Miccosukee, the U.S. forces encountered separate regiments of Native and Black Seminoles. Initially, the Seminoles offered resistance, but, outnumbered by at least 10 to 1, they had to scatter into the swamps and forest to avoid capture or death. Again, U.S. forces burned the houses and obtained supplies of livestock and grain. Also, they retrieved the white woman who was spared at the ambush of Lieutenant Scott's party.[26]

At Suwanee, another British agent, Robert Ambrister, was captured. Arbuthnot and Ambrister were both accused of playing roles in events that had occurred since the War of 1812. Under the supervision of General Gaines, a military court ordered Arbuthnot to be hanged and Ambrister to be executed by a firing squad.[27] The fates of Arbuthnot and Ambrister symbolically signaled the conclusion of the First Seminole War. Each had been charged by the United States with considerable responsibility at its beginning. Now their deaths should have brought the hostilities to a close, but this false reasoning was soon obvious. If the Seminoles had had no other cause for hostility, the elimination of men who had armed them and coaxed them to attack frontier settlements then should have brought any further depredations to a halt. But the correspondence between the secretary of war, and Generals Jackson and Gaines, revealed that declarations of victory were premature.[28]

Jackson had conducted his campaigns between February and April 1818. In May, he informed Calhoun of the continued black threat. Nevertheless, in July, President Monroe informed James Madison that Jackson still insisted the whole war could be blamed on British adventurers and on the Spanish.[29] Jackson's statements to Calhoun and Monroe seem to suggest undertones of duplicity among U.S. policymakers.

Because of Britain's interests in Florida, it was understandable that the British would seek to prevent U.S. expansion. Also, because the British were relatively weak, they would have a need to seek Seminole allies just as Spain had done. In his State of the Union Address, Monroe informed Congress that the Spanish government was bound by a 1795 treaty to prevent slaves from entering Florida and to control Seminole depredations. Monroe insisted that Spain's lack of authority provided a legal basis for Jackson's invasion.[30]

Jackson's effort in Florida eliminated the lingering British presence from the War of 1812 and the Spanish authority dating back to the 17th century. But his letter to Calhoun showed that key U.S. policymakers were extremely apprehensive about a Black Seminole resurgence. Therefore, while Monroe and Secretary of State Adams used existing problems with Britain and Spain as the key excuses in Congress and in diplomacy for the war, more confidential documentation indicates parallel efforts before, during, and after the war to circumscribe MLR.

Though Jackson had publicly declared victory, he and Gaines warned Calhoun to expect new attacks. In one letter to Calhoun, Jackson referred to Florida's instability: "[H]er territory will always prove an asylum to the disaffected and restless savage as well as to a more dangerous population, unless some energetic government can be established."[31] Jackson's comment reflects the dominant military perspective after the war. The Seminole problem, especially with the blacks, was not yet solved, and policymakers continued to grapple with it, but Monroe believed the war presented a prime opportunity for U.S. acquisition of Florida. With her colonies in revolt throughout the hemisphere, he reasoned that Spain could little afford to squander her fleeting power to maintain Florida.

Monroe believed that this apparently unending problem with the Black Seminoles should be used to finally achieve an American objective that he had struggled with at least since he had assisted Jefferson and Madison in negotiating the Louisiana Purchase. In 1795 the United States and Spain had signed the Treaty of San Lorenzo. Under article 5 of this treaty, Spain had agreed to forcibly restrain all Indians within Florida from attacking U.S. territory. Under article 6, Spain had agreed to return all runaway slaves.[32]

In December 1818, just after the First Seminole War, Monroe, in his State of the Union Address, said this on the Florida issue: "If the embarrassments of Spain prevented her from making an indemnity to citizens . . . for their losses by spoliation and otherwise, it was always in her power to have provided it by the cession of this territory. Of this her government has been repeatedly apprised . . . and would likewise relieve herself from the important obligation secured by the treaty of

1795 and all other compromitments [*sic*] respecting it."[33]

The United States had long sought to own Florida, and it seems that a combination of circumstances convinced Spain to take Monroe's advice. In February 1819, the Senate ratified the Washington Treaty, in which Spain ceded all its lands lying east of the Mississippi to the United States. Spain added some amendments that were finally ratified by the Senate in February 1821. Article 9 of the treaty required both nations to renounce all claims on each other. In article 11, the United States agreed to pay U.S. citizens $5 million for claims against Spain for property losses under the 1795 Treaty of San Lorenzo.[34] Monroe seemed to be angry over Spain's need for amendments to the treaty. In his State of the Union Address in December 1819, he said, "[T]he indemnity for... losses [of runaway slaves living in Florida] sustained, and now again acknowledged and provided for... was nevertheless received as the means of indemnifying our citizens in a considerable sum, the presumed amount of their losses."[35]

In the treaty by which the United States acquired Florida, Monroe used the strength of the Seminoles and the weakness of the Spanish to the advantage of the United States. Although Spain had agreed to return slaves and control the behavior of the Seminoles, the Patriots War re-established the African-Indian-Spanish alliance in the interests of the Spanish, natives, and blacks. Since the 1795 treaty, U.S. policymakers had reconciled themselves to the inability of Spain to enforce the agreement; however, the realliance in the Patriots War left them frustrated. The Negro fort provided a target that transcended the alliance and allowed the United States to attack the core problem threatening the South. The persistent threats of MLR, however, seemed to be the key factor or vehicle for Monroe's insistence on indemnity. MLR underscored the Spanish weakness in relation to the stipulations of the 1795 treaty. Although U.S. citizens had claims against Spain for a variety of issues, the claims of the slave industry stood out as the dominant point of contention that administrations since Washington's had imposed on the Spanish. Therefore, it seems likely that the claims of the slave industry were the quid pro quo that paid the price for Florida.

The acquisition of Florida provided the Monroe administration with the long sought opportunity to circumscribe the activities of MLR. The United States now provided the firm energetic government of which Jackson had spoken. The Monroe administration then initiated further steps that technically increased the control of the federal government over the lives and activities of the Black Seminoles.

In 1820, Secretary of War Calhoun appointed federal commissioners to assist Georgia state commissioners in gaining possession of the Black Seminoles for Georgia citizens. Using the provisions of the 1790 Treaty of New York, the 1796 Treaty of Colerain, and agreements between the state of Georgia and the Creek Indians, these commissioners were seeking to gain possession of the Black Seminoles and re-enslave them.[36]

At Indian Springs in 1820, the commissioners negotiated with a group of Creek chiefs. All of the past treaties had been negotiated by Creek leaders. Consequently, the Creeks were charged with failing to live up to the treaties because they had not delivered the Black Seminoles to their masters. Speaking for the Creek chiefs, McIntosh said that they had delivered the few blacks as had been required at various intervals since the Washington administration. He said that the British took many blacks and gave them a fort, and "we helped you destroy the fort." Also, McIntosh said, he had marched with General Jackson and had helped him catch blacks in the Seminole War. He reminded the commissioners that the blacks were living among the Seminoles, and hence their mutual adversary in the war. McIntosh concluded by declaring that the Upper Creeks had complied with all treaties.[37]

The commissioners responded to the Creeks:

We are however sorry to find that you do not consider yourselves bound to restore to us the property as well as the Negroes taken or destroyed by your nation before the Treaty of New York. . . . Brothers: We, your friends want nothing but what is right; but that we must insist upon. You were bound to restore all property taken from us. . . . In the Treaty of Augusta, thirty-seven years ago, you agreed to restore all Negroes, horses, cattle, or other property taken since the late war. By the treaty of Galphinton, thirty-five years ago, you agreed to restore all Negroes, horses, or other property. . . . In the Treaty of Shoulderbone, thirty-four years ago, you made the same promise. . . . By the Treaty of New York, you promised to restore all Negroes then in the nation belonging to the Georgians. . . . By the Treaty of Colerain you entered the same obligation. . . . Brothers: We know or have heard of very few Negroes having been returned or paid for . . . and our head man the Governor of Georgia has directed us to insist according to the laws of our country, upon the restoration of, or payment for, the increase of all such Negroes belonging to the people of Georgia as have increased.... As to Negroes now remaining among the Seminole, belonging to white people, we consider those people a part of the Creek nation; and we look to the Chiefs of the Creek nation to cause the people there... to do justice.[38]

The commissioners decided that the Creek nation was liable for previous generations of slaves who had escaped from Georgia. It seems probable that some claims went back as far as the colonial days. As compensation, the commissioners determined that the Creeks would forfeit the vast majority of their landholdings to the state of Georgia. Also, the Creeks owed the slave masters up to $250,000. This sum was to be paid by the federal government to the Georgians for the Creeks.[39] The following stipulation was added by Commissioners Daniel Forney of North Carolina and David Meriwhether of Georgia, and the former Georgia Governor David Mitchell, now U.S. agent for Indian affairs:

Whereas a treaty or convention has this day been made and entered into by and between the United States and the Creek Nation, by the provisions of which the United States have agreed to pay, and the commissioners of the State of Georgia have agreed to accept... for the discharge of all bona fide and liquidated claims which the citizens of the said state may establish against the Creek nation... and we do hereby assign, transfer, and set over unto the United States, for the use and benefit of the said Creek nation... all the rights, title, and interest of the citizens of the said state to all claims, debts, damages, and property, of every description.[40]

The Treaty of Indian Springs essentially gave the Monroe administration total legal control over all blacks in Florida. Although the treaty stipulated that, for the benefit of their Creek allies, the U.S. government was the legal owner of the Black Seminoles, if any Black Seminoles were captured, the U.S. government would exercise all administrative control. Negotiations between McIntosh and the commissioners suggest that the natives had little real say in the matter. Although the Upper Creeks had been faithful allies of the U.S. government, their land was taken with impunity. Monroe declared that Spain did not restrain its Indians as required under the 1795 treaty. These "Indians," of course, were the Black and Native Seminoles. Therefore, for the purpose of indemnifying Georgians, the Seminoles were the legal wards of Florida. Nevertheless, when McIntosh made the same point to show that the Black Seminoles were residents of Florida and were not to be counted among the Upper Creeks, the commissioners denied this statement. Without exercising such convenient duplicity in diplomacy, it was unlikely that the U.S. could have laid blame on the Creeks for the millions of dollars that southern slave holders had lost in slave property. To help provide the legal basis for the acquisition of Florida, Monroe had previously declared that the Black Seminoles were under Spanish authority and covered by the 1795 treaty. Thus, the Seminoles were to be controlled by Spain. But to acquire the bulk of remaining Creek lands for Georgia, Monroe declared the Seminoles to be governed by the Upper Creeks. The failure of all past treaties with Spain and the Creeks, therefore, became the legal basis for the 1819–21 Florida Treaty and the 1821 Indian Springs treaty.

However, the Indian Springs treaty was most revealing as a prediction of what the conflict was to evolve into. This treaty made the U.S. government *de jure* slave masters. Therefore, a battle would eventually ensue between slaves and slave masters.

The destruction of the Negro fort was specifically a confrontation of the United States with Black Seminoles. The comments of Gaines and Arbothnot suggest that Black Seminoles were the primary target of the First Seminole War. These two military initiatives were largely against MLR. The stipulations and diplomacy surrounding the treaties of 1819–21 suggest an effort to control MLR. Despite these efforts, American policymakers seemed to believe MLR was resurgent. The military threat of the Seminoles had not decreased in spite of the geopolitical efforts of the British and early American administrations to facilitate this objective.

Andrew Jackson was appointed the first governor of Florida in 1821, just after the treaties of that same year were ratified. In May, Monroe wrote Jackson, "I have full confidence that your appointment will be immediately and most beneficially felt. Smugglers and slave traders will hide their heads, pirates will disappear, and the Seminole cease to give us trouble."[41] This was only wishful thinking on the part of the president. By July, Jean Penieres, the subagent for Indian affairs in Florida, provided Jackson with a territorial review of land and inhabitants:

> We must add to this enumeration . . . fifty or sixty Negroes, or mulattos, who are maroons, or half slaves to the Indians. These Negroes appeared to me far more intelligent than those who are in absolute slavery; and they have great influence over the minds of the Indians. It will be difficult to form a prudent determination with respect to the maroon Negroes who live among the Indians on the other side of the little moun-

tains of Latchiove. Their number is said to be upward of three hundred. They fear again being made slaves under the American government and will omit nothing to increase or keep alive mistrust among the Indians, whom they in fact govern. If it should become necessary to use force with them, it is to be feared that the Indians will take their part. It will, however, be necessary to remove from Florida this lawless group of free booters, among whom runaway Negroes will always find refuge. It would perhaps be possible to have them received at St. Domingo, or furnish them the means of withdrawing themselves from the United States.[42]

The comments of Penieres reveal a general perception of instability in Florida. It seems that the military and political initiatives of the previous five years had done little to eliminate the threat that MLR posed to U.S. interests. Penieres said runaway slaves would always find refuge among the rebels; consequently, he saw no reason to believe that U.S. forces would prevail over MLR in Florida.[43] A U.S. conquest of this grand scale of rebellion would, of course, have brought the scope of this phenomenon back to a micro-level, and as such would not require national forces to oppose it. This macro-level of rebellion was facilitated by the runaway slaves' alliance with the Native Seminoles. The inability of the United States to formulate a military solution is emphasized by the discussion of sending the blacks to St. Domingo or other locations. Penieres believed that the Native Seminoles were governed by the Black Seminoles. At the core of this perception may have been a native-black alliance that dated back to the Yamasee War of 1714, or even to bonds established by Africans and Indians as fellow slaves and cimmaróns before 1700. Another explanation of this perception could be the diplomatic inventiveness of a desperate people. To remain free the rebels had to fight. To win on the battlefield against such powerful foes, they needed allies. To maintain alliances they had to be persuasive and influential as they related to these allies. Consequently, some observers mistakenly described influence as "governing."

At any rate, Penieres's advice soon was factored into national policy making. Jackson wrote Calhoun by September, "These runaway Negroes spoken of by Mr. Penieres must be removed from the Floridas or scenes of murder and confusion will exist and lead to unhappy consequences which cannot be controlled."[44]

Removing those blacks required the defeat of MLR. This had not been accomplished by U.S. forces. Therefore, Jackson's prophecies came true. In the Second Seminole War, Jackson would lead U.S. policymakers as president, crafting new political and military initiatives with hopes of ultimately ending the threat of the Black Seminoles. This time, U.S. policymakers would seek to destroy the ancient Seminole alliance.

Notes

1. *Annals of Congress*, vol. 4, 15th Cong., 2d sess., 19 February 1819, 256–57.

2. Covington, *Seminoles of Florida*, 34–42.

3. Mulroy, *Border*, 14–16.

4. *Am. St. P.*, 1, *Foreign Relations*, 4:547–51.

5. Ibid., 552–60.

6. *Annals of Congress*, vol. 2, 15th Cong., 2d sess., 15 August 1816, 1981.

7. Peters, *Florida Wars*, 22.

8. Giddings, *Exiles*, 32–34.

9. Ibid., 35–38; *Am. St. P.*, 1, *Foreign Relations*, 4:551–56.

10. *Annals of Congress*, vol. 4, 15th Cong., 2d sess., 23 April 1816, 1828.

11. *Am. St. P.*, 1, *Foreign Relations*, 4:556.

12. *Annals of Congress*, vol. 4, 15th Cong., 2d sess., 15 June 1816, 1974.

13. *Annals of Congress*, vol. 2, 15th Cong., 2d sess., 15 June 1816, 1973.

14. *Annals of Congress*, vol. 4, 15th Cong., 2d sess., 13 August 1816, 1978–81; Giddings, *Exiles*, 37–42; Peters, *Florida Wars*, 23–25.

15. Giddings, *Exiles*, 38.

16. John Quincy Adams, *Memoirs of John Quincy Adams*, vol. 4, ed. Charles Francis Adams (Philadelphia: J. B. Lippincott and Co., 1875), 179.

17. *Am. St. P.*, 5, *Military Affairs*, 1:681–87; Giddings, *Exiles*, 48; Caroline Mays Brevard, *A History of Florida* (Deland, Fla.: Florida Historical Society, 1924), 46.

18. *Am. St. P.*, 5, *Military Affairs*, 1:689; John C. Calhoun, *The Papers of John C. Calhoun*, vol. 2, 1817–1818, ed. W. Edwin Hemphill (Columbia, S.C.: University of South Carolina Press, 1963), 39; Monroe, *Writings*, vol. 6, 78.

19. *Am. St. P.*, 5, *Military Affairs*, 1:689.

20. *Annals of Congress*, vol. 3, 15th Cong., 2d sess., 27 January 1818, 2037.

21. *Annals of Congress*, vol. 2, 15th Cong., 2d sess., 21 February 1818, 2035.

22. Peters, *Florida Wars*, 51–52; Giddings, *Exiles*, 49, 50.

23. *Annals of Congress*, vol. 4, appendix, 15th Cong., 2d sess., 2295–96.

24. *Am. St. P.*, 5, *Military Affairs*, 1:691.

25. Ibid., 689–708; Giddings, *Exiles*, 50–55; Covington, *Seminoles of Florida*,

43–47; Peters, *Florida Wars*, 51–55.

26. Giddings, *Exiles*, 50–55; Covington, *Seminoles of Florida*, 43–47; *Am. St. P.*, 5, 1:689–708.

27. *Annals of Congress*, vol. 4, appendix, 15th Cong., 2d sess., 2062; Covington, *Seminoles of Florida*, 46–47.

28. Calhoun, *Papers*, vol. 3, 20, 143, 152, 184, 312.

29. Monroe, *Writings*, vol. 6, 53.

30. Ibid.

31. Calhoun, *Papers*, vol. 3, 313.

32. Miller, *Treaties*, vol. 2, 1776–1818, 318–23; Calhoun, *Papers*, vol. 3, 313.

33. Monroe, *Writings*, vol. 6, 77.

34. Miller, *Treaties*, vol. 3, 1819–1835, 3–12.

35. Monroe, *Writings*, vol. 6, 106.

36. *Am. St. P.*, 2, *Indian Affairs*, 2:249–51; Giddings, *Exiles*, 63–67.

37. *Am. St. P.*, 2, *Indian Affairs*, 2:252–53; Giddings, *Exiles*, 63–67.

38. *Am. St. P.*, 2, *Indian Affairs*, 2:253–56; Giddings, *Exiles*, 63–67.

39. Kappler, *Indian Affairs*, vol. 2, 195–98; *Am. St. P.*, 2, *Indian Affairs* 2:256.

40. Giddings, *Exiles*, 63–67; *Am. St. P.*, 2, *Indian Affairs*, 2:256.

41. Madison, *Writings*, vol. 6, 185

42. *Am. St. P.*, 2, *Indian Affairs*, 2:411.

43. Ibid., 414.

44. Ibid.

Section C

The Black Seminole Response

In 1693, the Black Seminoles became part of an alliance with the Spanish and various Native Americans. The United States eliminated the Spanish from this alliance in 1821. By 1834, President Andrew Jackson had attempted to further isolate the Black Seminoles with his order to send the Native Seminoles west and return the Black Seminoles to slavery. This order began the "Great Seminole War," or Second Seminole War, from which the Black Seminole Abraham emerged as perhaps the war's most dynamic and charismatic personality. Abraham came to symbolize the Black Seminoles' evolution from silent partners in a three-way alliance to dominant war policy negotiators with U.S. generals. The political significance of the Black Seminoles is apparent in the final chapter; they emerged as latent allies of abolitionist Congressmen Joshua Giddings and John Quincy Adams.

Chapter 7

The Second Seminole War, 1835–42*

The Second Seminole War, which occurred between 1835 and 1842, was a war initiated by the slave industry. Every American president between 1788 and 1836, except John Adams and John Quincy Adams, had been a slaveholder. Between 1836 and 1842, President Martin Van Buren, though not a slaveholder, favored the interests of slavery regarding the Second Seminole War.[1]

Only slave-holding presidents had held office for two terms. The tenures of both Adamses and Van Buren were one term each. Key policies concerning the Seminoles were shaped for slaveholders and in administrations dominated by slaveholders. Many slaveholders held key offices in Monroe's administration, but technically, under the Treaty of Indian Springs, the U.S. government itself became a slave-holding institution. Therefore, between the signing of the Indian Springs treaty in 1821 and the outbreak of the Second Seminole War in 1835, national policies on the Black Seminoles were truly dictated by the slave industry.

After 1821, President Monroe, Secretary of War Calhoun, and General Jackson had voiced apprehensions over the military and social cohesion between the Black and Native Seminoles. Black Seminoles particularly were still seen as a major threat to the slave industry, even though the federal government had technically become

---

* See figures C and D on pages 74 and 125.

their master and Florida was a U.S. territory. Consequently, a policy was initiated to separate the Seminoles. This policy called for the re-enslavement of the blacks, and U.S. attempts to execute it resulted in the Second Seminole War. However, this separation strategy failed. Therefore, MLR continued to survive, and the Black Seminoles achieved their policy objectives. We can trace U.S. policy initiatives and failures, as well as the success of the objectives of the Black Seminoles, by examining the Fort Moultrie Treaty, the Treaty of Payne's Landing, and the Articles of Capitulation. In the Second Seminole War, MLR became a dominant influence in Florida.

In 1821, the Florida Indian agent Penieres, Governor Andrew Jackson, and Secretary of War Calhoun communicated on the issue of the Black Seminole threat to the slave industry. By 1823, the Fort Moultrie Treaty was initiated. In this treaty, the U.S. government officially acknowledged the Seminoles as an independent Native American nation. An effort was made to place the Seminoles on a Florida reservation. Article 7 of the treaty stated the following: "The Chiefs and warriors aforesaid...stipulate to be active and vigilant in preventing the retreating to, or passing through, the district of country assigned them, of any absconding slaves, or fugitives from justice; and further agree, to use all necessary exertions to apprehend and deliver the same to the agent, who shall receive orders to compensate them agreeably to the trouble and expense incurred."[2]

The Fort Moultrie Treaty began to shape the circumstances under which the Second Seminole War would occur. As with the Creeks and the Spanish, a third party was made responsible for the Black Seminoles. Even though the Treaty of Indian Springs technically elim-inated all claims on the Black Seminoles, the erratic nature of the slave-catching system could make any blacks in Florida a retrievable commodity. All Black Seminoles were seen as suspect, and conse-quently, the presence of numerous blacks brought requests from the slave industry for compensation. The federal government provided bureaucrats from the Department of Indian Affairs to mediate between the claims of the U.S. slave industry and those of the Native Seminoles who also claimed some blacks as slaves.[3]

As the first U.S. governor of Florida, Jackson was acutely aware of the complexities of white and Indian claims on blacks living in Florida, and he informed Calhoun that the United States should not make treaties with a subject people. Jackson and Calhoun concurred in the idea of moving all eastern Indians west of the Mississippi River.[4] In

1824 Monroe told both houses of Congress that eastern Indians should be required to exchange their land for equal amounts west of the Mississippi.[5]

Before becoming president, Jackson believed that the federal government should not interfere with states' attacks on Indian treaties. Until the Jackson presidency, previous administrations grudgingly had acknowledged Indian sovereignty. However, as president, Jackson executed an Indian policy based on ideas expressed during the Monroe administration. In 1830, Congress passed the Indian Removal Act. This law forced all Indians east of the Mississippi to exchange their lands for western territory. Treaties were to be negotiated between individual tribes and the federal government to accomplish this end.[6]

In 1832, the Seminoles were forced to negotiate the Treaty of Payne's Landing, which required them to give up their Florida homes and move to Arkansas. They were granted two years to accomplish this task, but complications developed. The Seminoles refused to emigrate west. Article 6 of the treaty stated: "The Seminole being anxious to be relieved from the repeated vexatious demands for slaves, and other property, alleged to have been stolen and destroyed by them, so that they may remove unembarrassed to their new homes, the United States stipulate to have the same property investigated, and to liquidate such as may be satisfactorily established, provided the amount does not exceed seven thousand dollars."[7]

The Treaty of Indian Springs had theoretically erased the claims of southern slaveholders to the Black Seminoles, but in the years between 1821 and 1832, an indefinite number of black slaves had escaped to the Seminoles from Florida, Georgia, and Alabama. The slave industry was waiting to stake a claim and forcibly apprehend the blacks. Therefore, within the Seminole nation, a decision was made to resist removal as the only sure means of securing the Black Seminoles. President Jackson demanded that the Seminoles be forcibly removed and the blacks re-enslaved as stipulated in the Payne's Landing treaty. This series of events erupted into the catastrophic Second Seminole War in 1835.[8]

By 1834, it was evident that the Seminole chiefs had decided not to be removed. The Seminole Indian agent, General Wiley Thompson, told Secretary of War Lewis Cass that the chiefs said that they wanted to be near their ancestors' graves. Thompson, however, said that the Seminoles' fear of losing their black slaves was the real reason for their refusal to emigrate, and he informed the chiefs that they would have to part with their slaves anyway. Cass and Thompson believed that the Seminoles' refusal to emigrate was the idea of the blacks. Thompson requested troops to protect friendly chiefs because he believed that blacks and hostile Native Americans would kill any Seminole trying to emigrate.[9]

One of the stipulations in the Treaty of Payne's Landing was that the Seminoles, as Creeks, would be located on Creek land in Arkansas. In 1834, Florida Governor William Duval and Thompson informed the War Department that Black Seminoles knew Creeks would seek to claim them under stipulations of the 1821 Treaty of Indian Springs. Additionally, they said crooked whites, who sold whiskey to the Seminoles in exchange for their corn, sought to prevent their removal. Thompson wrote that "a third cause of hostility to emigration is the influence which it is said the Negroes, the very slaves in the nation, have over the Indians. The Negroes are more provident than the Indians. They not only often feed the hungry Indian but having the means they introduce by stealth into the nation sometimes considerable quantities of whiskey, which enable them while they derive a profit from the sale of it, to gratify the vitiated and intemperate appetite of the Indian. This gives them a controlling influence over him."[10]

As early as 1821, Penieres had informed Governor Andrew Jackson that the Black Seminoles "in fact govern" the Indians, and should be removed to St. Domingo. Jackson told Calhoun that if the blacks were not removed, uncontrollable devastation would occur.[11] Also, Duval wrote the Department of Indian Affairs: "Slaves belonging to the Indians have a controlling influence over their masters and are utterly opposed to any change of residence. No treaty can be enforced as long as these Blacks are present, every Indian who seeks to stay will run to them."[12]

Even before he executed his Indian removal philosophy into law, Andrew Jackson was apprehensive about the presence of Black Seminoles in Florida. There was a perception in the U.S. Department of War that, although many blacks were slaves of the Indians, the blacks nonetheless controlled them. The implication seemed to be that blacks used this control to block the execution of federal laws and that they threatened to kill Native Seminoles who sought to cooperate with the government. Slavery and other relations between Black and Native Seminoles were reviewed in the first chapter.

The very notion of masters being ruled by slaves is contradictory. Nonetheless, its documentation within the War Department was previously confirmed. If indeed blacks were a controlling force in the

Seminole nation and were able to orchestrate death threats, then perhaps they were not actually slaves. Slavery requires the complete subjugation of master over slave. This prerequisite appears to have been missing among the Seminoles.

The primary rebel leader and one of the most dominant, in general, was Abraham. Abraham served as the interpreter for the Seminoles during negotiations for the Treaty of Payne's Landing. He had at one time been known as the slave of the principal Seminole chief and had acted as his prime minister. Abraham accompanied the chiefs to Washington in 1825–26 as interpreter.[13] One U.S. commander of the Florida war, General Jesup, described Abraham as "[t]he principal Negro chief, supposed to be friendly to the whites; said to be a good soldier and an intrepid leader; he is the most cunning and intelligent Negro we have seen; he is married to the widow of the former chief of the nation."[14]

The Treaty of Payne's Landing required Abraham and other Seminole leaders to travel to Arkansas and review the Creek lands they would share. Abraham made two memorable determinations in the treaty. First, the Florida Indian agent had become financially indebted to Abraham; therefore, Abraham added a stipulation to the treaty that required financial compensation for interpreters. Second, and most important, Abraham required that the Seminoles be granted land separate from the Creeks because of the Creeks' claims on blacks.[15] Regarding treaty negotiations, John T. Sprague said, "The mischievous influences of the whites, through the [b]lack interpreters, operating upon the malignity and suspicions of the younger class of Indians, nearly defeated the object."[16] From the Seminole perspective the clauses stipulated by Abraham were binding. The Jackson administration insisted that the Seminoles were required to emigrate regardless of the desires of the chiefs and the people. The Seminole leaders insisted that emigration was required only if all Seminoles were satisfied.

The 24th Congress required President Jackson to submit a report detailing the causes of the Second Seminole War. Secretary of War Cass noted that all problems began when the administration decided troops were needed to enforce the Treaty of Payne's Landing. In early 1834, 94 prominent Florida citizens signed a letter to President Jackson demanding a solution to the problem of 500 runaway slaves among the Seminoles. Shortly afterward, federal troops moved in. Florida and Georgia slave catchers made constant efforts to seize undefended blacks. Clashes between settlers and Seminoles increased.[17] By January 1835, the War Department decided to escalate its efforts to force removal, and it wanted to provide increased security for settlers. Consequently, General Scott was put in command of the U.S. Army in Florida. Secretary of War Cass said, "General Scott was directed to allow no pacification with the Indians while a living slave belonging to a white man remained in their possession."[18]

As the situation in Florida intensified, Abraham gave the U.S. authorities the impression that he was in favor of enforcing the treaty, and yet he planned for war. From Havana fishermen, he received shipments of gunpowder and other arms, and he secretly notified plantation blacks to revolt when war broke out. Even Major Francis Dade, the greatest casualty of the war, believed until his death that Abraham was peaceful.[19]

General Scott demanded that the Seminole chiefs assemble their people for emigration, but Abraham and the Native American chief Osceola threatened to kill any chief who cooperated. When Chief Mathala assembled his people to go, he was killed. In an effort to coordinate the military pressure on the Seminoles for removal, 110 men under Major Dade sailed into Tampa Bay from New Orleans. A plantation slave in Tampa, Louis Pacheco, was selected to lead Dade 130 miles north to Fort King. Pacheco notified the Seminoles of his route, and Dade's entire command, except for two men who escaped, were ambushed and killed. Abraham and 80 warriors participated in the attack along with approximately 120 other Seminoles.[20]

At about the same time that Major Dade met his fate, General Thompson and several others were ambushed and scalped by Osceola and about 20 warriors.[21] The attacks on Dade and Thompson formally inaugurated the war. The Treaty of Payne's Landing left two options for the Black Seminoles: to prevail on the battlefield, or to return to plantation slavery. It was this choice that spurred Abraham's violent response. As a leading member of the Seminole nation and a diplomat, Abraham had traveled to Washington, D.C., and he was well aware of the power and wealth of the United States. He knew that, ultimately, the Seminoles could not prevail. Nonetheless, his objective was to wage such a protracted guerrilla struggle that U.S. political and military leaders would be forced to alter the treaty to provide better terms for the blacks. Abraham sought either the right to remain in Florida or free passage for all blacks to Arkansas and land separate from the Creeks.[22]

A few weeks after the massacre of Dade's forces, citizens of St. Augustine gathered to prepare to defend the city. They sent a message of distress to Congress, the president, and southern newspapers stating: "Our delegate requested to urge upon the Congress...and upon the President the early consideration of calamities and ruin...by the ravages of an unrestrained savage foe. Now just conceive their position—eight hundred or one thousand warriors...with three or four hundred Negroes of their own, better disciplined and more intelligent than themselves, to whom there is a daily accession of runaway Negroes from the plantations."[23]

Even though many Indians such as Osceola were violently opposed to emigration, the treaty held out options for them that most seemed willing to accept. The Second Seminole War was a war to preserve the freedom of the Black Seminoles. Abraham personified the struggle politically and militarily. As the Spanish, then Indian, pretexts were removed by diplomacy, the federal government was able to legally and politically circumscribe the Black Seminoles. The Treaty of Payne's Landing left the Black Seminoles politically and legally isolated. However, the United States was ill prepared to confront the strongest aspect of MLR, the blacks' guerrilla military alliance with the Indians. Equally important to the survival of MLR was the theater of operations—the jungles, swamps, and forests of Florida. As MLR transcended all pretext, in a mode of self-preservation Abraham stepped from the background to assume a dominant political and military role. With the fate of all Black Seminoles at stake, this was only appropriate.

After the Dade massacre, full-scale military operations got under way. General Winfield Scott was in command, assisted by Generals Duncan Clinch, Abraham Eustis, Edmund Gaines, and Thomas Jesup. There were approximately 6,000 U.S. troops and 500 to 1,000 Seminoles. General Gaines was ordered to proceed from Tampa and retrace Dade's route with about 1,200 troops. En route, Gaines was attacked by the Seminoles on the Withlacoochee River. Gaines estimated that he was confronted by 1,200 to 1,500 Seminoles. Several of his men were killed in an assault that seemed to come from all directions. The Seminoles burned the forests to confuse Gaines. U.S. forces were pinned down for more than a week. They got low on ammunition and began to slaughter horses for food. They even ate a dog. Gaines sent a rider for help. At last, Abraham came forward and called a truce. He requested brandy and tobacco and allowed the Americans to fish in the river. In later negotiations, both sides agreed to stay on their own sides of the river. Fearing starvation and a massacre, Gaines told the Seminoles to beware because vast U.S. forces would arrive any day. Finally, General Clinch arrived and the Seminoles fled.[24]

Between December and June, 1835–36, numerous battles occurred between the United States and the Seminoles. In most instances, the Seminoles were outnumbered by 5 or 10 to 1. U.S. generals sent reports of victories against the enemy and noted how the Seminoles were dispersed from the battlefield, but they made little progress. Florida citizens were so fearful that they abandoned their plantations and sought refuge in forts and towns. The failure of U.S. troops on the battlefield spread consternation from Florida to the White House. In Tallahassee, the commander of U.S. troops, General Scott, was burned in effigy by the citizens. Florida Congressman Joseph White demanded that Scott be removed and that an investigation be held on the progress of the war.[25]

Captain John T. Sprague participated in many of the Florida battles and was in the theater essentially from beginning to end. Sprague described the general situation in Florida in 1836:

> The theatre of operations was a wilderness, and every hammock and swamp a citadel for the enemy.... They [the Seminoles] harassed the troops day and night, and with the fleetness of the deer, retired to a more secluded spot. The men, worn down with constant watchings, disappointments, and tedious marches, still no nearer the enemy, struggled on in hopes they would hazard a general action. Too wary for this they [the Seminoles] knew their strength consisted in moving in parties of 10, 15, or 20 men. Subsequent events, and the experience of intelligent officers, as well as citizens, have proved that a Florida campaign, however well timed, skillful and judicious in its arrangements and progress, was not to result in the capture or subjection of the Seminole.[26]

By mid-1836 it was apparent that the Seminoles who had fought removal, seeking better terms, were not defeated. Their guerrilla tactics were successful at thwarting armies 10 times their size. Their battlefield success set off a chain reaction. The War Department ordered Scott to remove the Seminoles and to offer no peace as long as slaves belonging to whites remained among them. This policy was unenforceable. It was initiated by slave-holding citizens pressuring Jackson, who then sent troops via the secretary of war to execute the policy. The utter failure of the policy reverberated in the executive and legislative branches of government. General Scott was essentially accused of incompetence. In June 1836, President Jackson convened a court of inquiry, as requested by the Senate, to discover what was going on in Florida.[27] Letters were circulating in the media casting blame on Scott's conduct. The president responded:

Who gave Genl [*sic*] Scott, Genl Jesup's letter will be a subject of Inquiry when I return—however it is immaterial—the delay of Genl Scott at Columbus, with his unaccountable order to Jessup [*sic*] to halt when near the Indians, when one hour's delay may have been the cause of the Indians' escape was sufficient proof of his want to capacity to fight Indians, and was sufficient ground to call him from the command against Indians. . . . Scott ought to have retired and not obtruded himself on the command assigned to Jesup, but when he did he ought to have acted with promptness and put this puny Indian war down in 10 days. General Scott had ought to know, I had no hostile feelings towards him—the shameful proceedings in Florida with the panic that pervaded everywhere, which has tarnished the reputation of our army ought to have induced every military man to have exerted themselves to have regained the army's lost military character. The Inquiry will be, has Genl Scott so acted[;] if so, he will stand acquitted, if not, he will stand condemned.[28]

The testimony presented in the inquiry revealed how a policy that was crafted in Washington became undone by guerrilla warfare. According to General James Gadsden, the U.S. troops were not prepared to fight a guerrilla war. He said, "[T]he contest on our part degenerated, and therefore, from a war to a hunt, in which the enemy had to be sought as you would seek the lion or the tiger, with the hazard of being sprung upon from every jungle or thicket."[29]

Colonel William Lindsay reported that the U.S. forces had as little knowledge of the theater as they had of the interior of Africa. He added that quicker than U.S. troops could erect tents, the Seminoles could construct a shelter from palmetto branches, which kept out rain.[30] General Eustis said he never encountered more than 50 Seminoles and that "the enemy was gifted with ubiquity, he was to be found everywhere and nowhere." Eustis reported that one-third of his 1,600 South Carolina volunteers contracted the measles.[31]

The inquiry, testimony, and disputes centered on Gaines's battle and subsequent negotiations with Abraham on the Withlacoochee River. Captain Thistle was pinned down with General Gaines at the Battle of Withlacoochee. Thistle testified that he assumed that they were confronted by 1,200 Indians and blacks. Thistle noted that they were out of food and were eating horses and dogs and were low on ammunition. He said, "The Negro Abraham hailed the camp," seeking peace, tobacco, and brandy; but in retrospect, Thistle believed that Abraham tricked Gaines, that he sought intelligence so the Seminole women and children could be moved away from the war.[32]

General Scott felt indignant at even having to appear. Scott was sure that Jackson, Gaines, and Jesup had some personal dislike of him and believed that the inquiry was a waste of time while his men were still fighting. He resented the term "failure of the Seminole campaign" and quickly pointed out that no one else had had any success in Florida.

The testimony of Scott and the inquiry in which it was solicited are explicitly demonstrative of Clausewitz's treatise on war and politics. According to Clausewitz, "[W]ar is not merely a political act, but also a real political instrument, a continuation of political commerce."[33] Considering Clausewitz, we see that the battlefield is transformed by definition into a quasi-legislative arena. In the case of the Seminole War, the theater, with its lack of success, was an arena ripe for the conception of policy alteration. The battle on the Withlacoochee River symbolizes the general failure of policy. In defending his Florida command, General Scott was a representative from this quasi legislature. As such, Scott was the first of many generals who, while accounting for failure in battle, became advocates or representatives for the general Seminole goals. The goals, of course, were specifically tied to Abraham's battlefield strategy and diplomatic forays. Abraham's personal security was never in doubt; he, therefore, endeavored for the masses of the Black Seminoles.

Scott and the succeeding commanders and other generals were the representatives, or quasi diplomats, from the battlefield who could not enforce policy and consequently could not convince U.S. policymakers to change policy. The inquiry was the beginning of the documented failure of U.S. policy goals and reciprocally, the documented reason to yield to the Seminoles (see figure D).

Scott defensively reviewed previous testimony: "I am persuaded that the total force of Seminole doesn't exceed 1,200. We've never yet seen 130, and I don't think 500 exist within 10 square miles, but parties of 10 to 30 are seen everywhere."[34]

Scott, sure that Gaines had been tricked by the Seminoles into revealing valuable intelligence, observed: "How was I, Mr. President, to account for our not finding, three weeks after General Gaines, any considerable body of the enemy? He supposed himself to be surrounded in his breastwork, with his 1,000 or 1,100 men, by 1,200 or 1,500 warriors. What had become of them? He certainly killed but few and captured not one. Whence then the subsequent dispersion?"[35]

Gaines had reported subduing and dispersing the Seminoles at Withlacoochee, but Scott noted that their request for brandy and

Figure D – How Policy Goals Moved to and from the Battlefield/Quasi Legislature

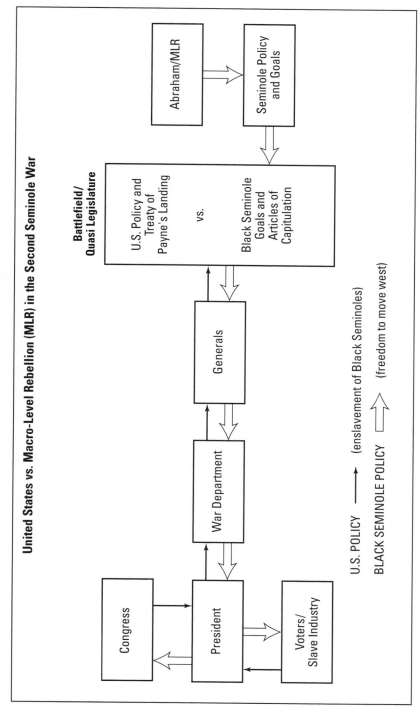

United States vs. Macro–Level Rebellion (MLR) in the Second Seminole War

tobacco was not the talk of a subdued enemy. Contrary to Gaines's report, Scott declared the Seminoles victorious.[36] He concluded that failure was caused by heat, sickness, and geography and that he "had not a guide that knew any intricacies of the 'cove,' a certain labyrinth, held from the knowledge of white man, as the sacred groves of the Druids were never entered except by the initiated.... Government gave me no topographical information, nor had any to give; and the booksellers' maps only... filled up with unlucky guesses."[37]

Scott endeavored to show that the fate of his campaign in Florida was not in his control. His testimony suggests that Gaines may have been pinned down for two weeks and nearly starved by a force one-tenth the size of his own. This mystery hints at a type of psychological warfare. The court of inquiry essentially cleared Scott and noted that U.S. forces were stalemated by the season, geography, and poor transportation.[38]

Nonetheless, Scott was removed from the Florida command. General Richard Call temporarily replaced him, and by November 1836, General Jesup was in command. Jesup zealously waged war against the Seminoles and sought to enforce the Treaty of Payne's Landing, but this agenda led him to become the chief advocate of the goals of Abraham and the Seminoles. After receiving his orders to command, Jesup wrote to Acting Secretary of War Benjamin Butler: "If I should not succeed in dislodging Powell, I can on returning to this place, strike Micanopy, Philip, and Cooper... each with from one hundred and twenty to two hundred Indians and Negro warriors, the latter perhaps the more numerous.... [T]his you may be assured is a Negro, not an Indian war; and if it be not speedily put down, the South will feel the effects of it on their slave population."[39]

Jesup served as commander of U.S. forces in Florida from November 1836 to July 1838. During this period he had limited success. He was able to reduce the total Seminole population in Florida by two-thirds after negotiations with Abraham; however, he could not change the general pattern that led to U.S. failure. To the end, until acceptable terms were achieved allowing all Seminoles to freely emigrate, they would move in deadly parties of three, four, or five, eluding U.S. forces 10 or 20 times their number.

It seems that Jesup had no illusions about the nature of the Seminole War. Though he did not specifically call it a slave-catching expedition or a war for the slave industry, Jesup recognized that slavery was the central issue. His conduct in the theater seemed to evolve from first identifying the real issues to advocating a solution, and then unilaterally executing that solution.

After putting Jesup in command, President Jackson remarked: "It is true that the whole Florida War from the first to the present time has been a succession of blunders and misfortune.... Everything at present is wrong.... I have tried all the Generals and as Genl Jesup is now there and in command, he I hope will finish this unfortunate business."[40] Jackson, surprisingly, seemed baffled by the tremendous difficulties in Florida. Because he had commanded during the First Seminole War, though, he was well aware of the difficulties inherent in declaring victory in Florida.

With 8,000 men, Jesup chased the Seminoles, from the Okefenokee Swamp of Georgia to the Everglades of Florida, still unable to subdue them. When tired or nearly cornered, the Seminoles sometimes declared truces as a ploy to regain their advantage. After months of heavy fighting, Jesup received peace overtures from Abraham. He wrote the secretary of war:

> I am awaiting most anxiously the movement of hostile chiefs, many of them prefer death to removal. In all the numerous battles and skirmishes that have taken place, not a single first-rate warrior has been captured.... The warriors have fought as long as they had life, and such seems to me, to be the determination of those who influence their councils—I mean the leading Negroes.... We may conquer them in time, and may destroy them, it is true; but the war will be a most harassing one.... I am not disposed to overrate the difficulties which surround me, but in communicating with you, it would be criminal to underrate them.... Abraham has just come in with a flag, accompanied by a nephew of the Indian Cloud, and a Negro chief.[41]

Perhaps sensing that U.S. forces were ready to alter their policy, Abraham and the key Seminole chiefs signed the Articles of Capitulation in March 1837. The articles incorporated the Payne's Landing stipulations except for one key change. Article 5 stated, "Major General Jesup, in behalf of the United States, agrees that the Seminole and their allies, who come in and emigrate to the west, shall be secure in their lives and property; that their Negroes their bona fide property, shall accompany them west."[42]

The Articles of Capitulation were never officially accepted by President Van Buren or the War Department. Officially, the U.S. Army in Florida still labored under President Jackson's orders to move Native

Seminoles west and return Blacks to slavery. It seems that the War Department accepted the battlefield realities as stated by Jesup and tacitly allowed him to pursue the policy as a battlefield necessity. Viewed together with the above statements of General Jesup, the articles reveal an army in the field that was growing weary of the Seminole War. Jesup indicates that little progress had been made toward success. The utter frustration of every battlefield effort caused the Payne's Landing treaty to be repudiated. Jesup had received unachievable orders. Therefore, he was trapped between an unyielding federal government and Seminole guerrillas who were apparently unbeatable. Abraham negotiated a solution to the problem. In exchange for Jesup's sincere efforts to enforce article 5, Abraham tirelessly sought to end the war and get all Seminoles to emigrate.[43] This compromise was a victory for MLR. The triumph of the guerrilla struggle had initiated a policy change.

Jesup wrote to Adjutant General Roger Jones that he would begin to disband his troops, that settlers could begin to return, and that the war was over. However, he noted, "A trifling impropriety on the part of the white population of the frontier might light it up again. The Negroes rule the Indians, and it is important they should feel themselves secure; if they should become alarmed and hold out, the war will be renewed."[44]

When news of Jesup's Articles of Capitulation reached the regional planters, who claimed Black Seminoles as their property, they wrote the War Department and their congressional representatives demanding that there be no peace until their slaves were apprehended. Jesup hoped that the more recent runaways would be surrendered by the Seminoles. To this end the wording of article 5 may have been intentionally ambiguous. In all probability, Abraham hoped to give as broad an interpretation to the words "allies" and "their Negroes their bona fide property" as possible to include all blacks among the Seminoles.

Jesup was pressured by the slave industry through the War Department and by battlefield realities. He probably hoped to let Abraham and enough of the other key Seminoles go west to bring about a beneficial effect on the battlefield. The slaveholders feared Jesup might somehow ignore orders from Washington and allow blacks to emigrate. Jesup had designated certain forts as sites where the Seminoles could surrender before being transported to Tampa and Arkansas. By May, Jesup reported to the War Department that the arrival of slaveowners at the evacuation sites had caused the blacks to flee. He insisted that because the "Negroes rule them," the Indians fled, too. This development was the cause of the war's renewal.[45]

Jesup had informed the War Department of the direct connection between free emigration of blacks and the end of hostilities. In spite of this communication, it seems that the War Department made no effort to prevent slaveholders from jeopardizing the freedom of the blacks. In June, Jesup informed Adjutant General Jones:

> I have the honor to report that this campaign, so far as relates to Indian emigration, has entirely failed. The Seminole chiefs were, I believe, sincere in their intentions of fulfilling the provisions of the treaty, but they have no influence over their people. . . . [T]hey were to have come in again on the 2nd, but failed, and on the night of that day they were seized by a force of armed warriors and removed to the interior. In the meantime, I desire you to present my most earnest request to the Secretary of War and the General in Chief that I be immediately relieved from command of this army.[46]

General Jesup was frustrated by his dilemma. The administration was continuing to yield to pressures from American noncombatants, who made his orders impossible to carry out. Jesup informed Adjutant General Jones in Washington:

> As an act of justice to all my predecessors in command, I consider it my duty to say, that the difficulties attending military operations in this country can be properly appreciated only by those acquainted with them. This is a service which no man would seek with any other view than the mere performance of his duty: distinction, or increase of reputation is out of the question; and the difficulties are such that the best concerted plans may result in absolute failure, and the best established reputation be lost without a fault. If I have at any time, said aught in disparagement of the operations of others, in Florida, either verbally or in writing, officially or unofficially, knowing the country as I now know it, I consider myself bound, as a man of honor, solemnly to retract it.[47]

Jesup had sent a letter to the press critical of General Scott that helped to spark a court of inquiry, but now, after several months of command and not really defeated but unable to win, he understood Scott's quandary. All the pressures of an impossible task had fallen on the military officers. He had already attempted to end the war on terms that benefited no one except the Black Seminoles. However, with the failure of this effort he now had to take his men back into a quagmire.

In a letter to Secretary of War Joel Poinsett, Jesup began to advocate the modification of the war policy:

> From the facts that are daily coming to my knowledge, I doubt whether the chiefs could exercise sufficient influence over their people to induce

any considerable portion of them to leave the country; and if they determine to remain, it will depend upon themselves how long they will remain; they cannot be driven out so long as they can obtain ammunition, unless we use northern Indians and Spanish bloodhounds. We may harass them, and ultimately destroy them, but it will cost as much time and treasure as the war carried on by the British government against the Maroons... [T]hat war, if I remember right, was terminated by the bloodhounds; and resulted not in unconditional submission but in a treaty which secured both liberty and property to the conquered. How far such a policy would be proper in the present case I am hardly prepared to give an opinion. The question is surrounded by difficulties, view it as you will. The two races, the Negro and the Indian, are rapidly approximating; they are identified in interests and feelings.... At the battle of Wahoo, a Negro, the property of a Florida planter, was one of the most distinguished leaders.... The depredations committed on the plantations east of the St. John's were perpetrated by the plantation Negroes, headed by an Indian Negro, John Cesar, since killed, and aided by some six or seven vagabond Indians.... I throw out these hints for the consideration of my official superiors, without pretending to offer an opinion as to the propriety of adopting them.[48]

Jesup's frustrations are perceivable in the letter to Poinsett. He underscored the impossibility of military victory. His plan of using bloodhounds was attempted, but it failed utterly.[49] Jesup showed signs of a battlefield political reaction, though. After rejecting the propriety of continuing to execute U.S. policy, he suggested freedom and land for the Seminoles, offerings that had already been made to the Indians in the Treaty of Payne's Landing. Therefore, he was advocating the interests of MLR. Also, Jesup explained that the blacks and Indians had the common bond of oppression and were formidable as battlefield allies in Florida. He verified that Abraham's battlefield strategy of gaining the allegiance of plantation blacks had had some success. The key point is Jesup's not-so-subtle advocacy for the goals of Abraham and MLR. Parallels drawn to the maroons, most likely of Jamaica, underscore the extent to which the Seminole War was a "Negro war," as specifically stated by Jesup.

Jesup commanded U.S. troops in Florida longer than did any other general, from November 1836 to July 1838. General Scott's inability to defeat the Seminoles had led to his dismissal. General Jesup, during his command, had succeeded in removing approximately 2,400 Seminoles to Arkansas.[50] He succeeded in this endeavor only after he had won the allegiance of Abraham and the official concurrence of key Native Seminole chiefs. Once the Articles of Capitulation had been signed, a ray of hope existed for the key instigators, the Black Seminoles. During the negotiation of the articles, Abraham's family and many other Native and Black Seminoles surrendered for removal. Jesup held Abraham's family hostage. The white planters caused most of the Seminoles to flee and resume hostilities, but with his family being held as hostages, Abraham consented to assist Jesup in an intensive diplomatic effort. With Abraham as a guide and diplomat, many Seminoles were captured and convinced to surrender. Often, women and children were captured as a prelude to the surrender of the warriors.[51]

According to Kenneth W. Porter, Jesup launched "a joint campaign of military operations and peace-propaganda."[52] Under this strategy, perhaps 400 (mostly noncombatant) blacks were returned to slavery. Most of these seem to have been recent runaways. At times, whole Seminole villages were captured while U.S. officers gained the Seminoles' trust under the white flag of peace. This tactic corresponds to the Seminole tactic of raising the white flag under the guise of peace, only to rest, move families, and get supplies from U.S. negotiators.

Nonetheless, though Jesup used tactics that violated truces and otherwise were duplicitous, he must be credited with a battlefield conversion which altered the course of history. First, he tried to yield totally to Abraham's goal; when this failed, he enforced the original policy of the War Department but modified the strategy. He sought freedom for the "bona fide property" of the Indians but re-enslavement for the most recent runaways. This modification grew into a policy that appeased the fears of the Seminoles and eventually halted the war.

In spite of removing two-thirds of the Seminoles, neither Jesup nor the War Department felt any less apprehensive about confronting the remaining warriors. Jesup remarked in a letter to the War Department, "We have at no former period of our history had to contend with so formidable an enemy. . . . Governor Coppinger is said to have expressed the opinion many years ago, that the Captain General of Cuba had not force enough to control the Seminole."[53]

During this period General Zachary Taylor confronted the Seminoles in what was probably the greatest battle of the war. Taylor, with about 1,200 men, faced approximately 250 Seminoles. Taylor chased the Seminoles 140 miles into the Everglades, where his men were forced to dismount and wade into a deep swamp to continue pursuit. While U.S. forces were in the swamp, the Seminoles poured a heavy barrage of fire on them, after which they retreated to the shores of Lake Okechobee. In his report to the War Department, Taylor's refrain follows those of Scott and Jesup before him:

> The action was a severe one, and continued from half-past twelve until three pm, a part of the time very close and severe. We suffered much, having twenty-six men killed and one-hundred and twelve wounded, among whom are some of our most valuable officers. . . . And here, I trust, I may be permitted to say, that I experienced one of the most trying scenes of my life, and he who could have looked on it with indifference, his nerves must have been very differently organized from my own—besides the killed, among whom were some of my personal friends, there lay one hundred and twelve wounded officers and soldiers, who had accompanied me one hundred and forty-five miles, most of the way through an unexplored wilderness . . . gallantly beaten the enemy, under my orders, in his strongest position, and who had to be conveyed back through swamps and hammocks. . . . Could the enemy be brought to battle, even in his strong holds, the war would soon be closed, no matter at what sacrifice of life on the part of officers and soldiers. . . . Fortunately for them, however that such is the nature of their country that concealment is found to be more efficacious than opposition, and they leave the climate to fight their battles. . . . [I]f nature has so organized the Indian that he is fleeter of foot than the white man, and given him a country where no tracks are left when he flies; and if we have not overtaken him, it is our misfortune, not our fault. And should the war be renewed (which I sincerely hope may never be the case) the only way to bring it to a successful issue, in my opinion, is to cover the whole country so as to prevent the enemy from hunting and fishing.[54]

In this communication, Taylor exhibits the same pattern of dispersing the enemy, but not defeating him, that Jesup described. This battle was the war's most direct confrontation, yet only 11 Seminoles were killed and none captured. Like Jesup, Taylor appears exasperated by an impossible mission. However, the boldness of Taylor's action prompted Jesup to pursue the Seminoles. In early 1838, Jesup chased the Seminoles into a swamp. He had 500 mounted men against perhaps 100 Seminoles. Jesup's men sustained 7 dead, 30 wounded. Jesup himself was severely wounded. No Seminoles were left on the field, so it is unknown whether they sustained any dead or wounded. General Eaton, Colonel Twiggs, and others of his men urged Jesup to end the fighting and let the Seminoles live in peace. Jesup concurred and sent a messenger to notify the Seminoles of the truce.[55]

In February 1838, Jesup made a final appeal to the War Department to modify its terms of surrender to the Seminoles. He sought a reservation for the Seminoles in Florida because of the impossibility of prevailing on the battlefield against them. According to Jesup, the lands were not yet needed by whites, and they would never be able to inhabit the region because of its climate. Jesup notified Secretary of War Poinsett that southern Florida was not worth the cost of the medicines needed in the campaigns. Jesup said:

> As a soldier it is my duty, I am aware, not to comment upon the policy of the government, but to carry it out in accordance with my instructions. I have endeavored faithfully to do so; but the prospect of terminating the war, in any reasonable time is anything but flattering. My decided opinion is, that unless immediate emigration be abandoned, the war will continue for years to come, and at constantly accumulating expense. Is it not then well worthy the serious consideration of an enlightened government, whether... the object we are contending for would be worth the cost[?] ... I respectfully recommend the measure to your consideration, and that of the President, as the only means of terminating, immediately, a most disastrous war, and leaving the troops disposable for other service. I desire a decision as soon as your convenience will permit, as by the middle of April at farthest, the troops must be withdrawn from the posts in the interior, to preserve their lives.[56]

Jesup was well aware of the Black Seminoles' quest to remain free and of their strategy to wage guerrilla war until freedom was ensured. He, therefore, advocated conditions under which freedom could reasonably be hoped for. However, Poinsett notified Jesup that only a temporary truce could be agreed to and that the Payne's Landing treaty had to be enforced. Jesup continued his dual strategy of war and negotiation, but by July, he had retired from Florida; after his departure, the Senate requested a report.[57] In that report, Jesup told the Senate that as commander in chief of the Army in the field, he felt that it was in his power to establish policies that would be most successful, but that he made sure that the ultimate decision was left to his superiors. Here it seems that Jesup was communicating a policy that contradicted his superiors, one that had been initiated by Abraham before hostilities but communicated to Jesup in the quasi legislature of the battlefield. Jesup told the Senate that without his policy modifications it was doubtful that "twenty warriors could have been killed or taken."[58]

Thus, Jesup retired from command of the Florida war. After having helped to ridicule General Scott for his lack of success, Jesup finally understood that the climate and geography of Florida, combined with the guerrilla tactics of the Seminoles, were more than a match for U.S. forces, who outnumbered them 10 to 1 and who possessed vast resources and technology. After making these discoveries, Jesup advocated the interests of the Seminoles as a means of terminating an endless war. His key partner in the modification of policy and battlefield diplomacy was the "intrepid" warrior, Abraham.

As Jesup prepared for retirement, he sent Abraham, his family, and approximately 90 other Black Seminoles to Arkansas. Before his departure, Abraham had a letter sent to Jesup with his X:

> I have the honor to present my best respects to you. Myself and Tony Barnet have done everything promised by us, and expect the General will do by us as he said at the beginning of this campaign. . . . We wish to get in writing from the General, the agreement made with us. We will go with the Indians to our new home, and wish to know how we are to be protected, and who is to have the care of us on the road. We do not live for ourselves only, but for our wives and children who are as dear to us as those of any other men. . . . I have charge of all the Red people coming on to Pease's Creek, and all are satisfied to go to Arkansas. . . . Whoever is to be Chief Interpreter we would wish to know. I cannot do any more than I have. I have done all I can, my heart has been true since I came in. . . . I hope Toskeegee is satisfied. All his Seminole Brethren are coming in. . . . All the Black people are contented I hope. Your servant Abraham.[59]

After nearly three years of warfare, the effort to enforce the Payne's Landing treaty was stalemated. But as Jesup and Abraham prepared to exit the theater, there was room for optimism. By this time, only the Washington policymakers and the slave industry that spurred them on still insisted on the re-enslavement of Black Seminoles and the removal of the Native Seminoles. In 1837, Jesup had begun to use Choctaw, Creek, and Delaware soldiers of fortune. He promised them and volunteer troops from the southern states a share of Seminole horses, cattle, slaves, and other plunder as partial payment for their services. On one campaign, many blacks, primarily women and children, were captured. All the soldiers of fortune and other claimants from the slave industry wanted a share of those slaves.

Jesup allowed a few of them to be sent into slavery with the white southern claimants. The rest were sent with Abraham to Fort Pike in New Orleans. Jesup required the Creeks and other Indians to be paid a bounty of $25 each as their share for claims on the Black Seminoles. This policy was endorsed by the secretary of war and the president in 1837.[60] As was the case with the Treaty of Indian Springs, these Seminoles became the property of the federal government. In this single case, Jesup uncovered the solution to ending the Seminole War. Here, he executed the original policy and initiated what would prove to be a permanent solution: He let 35 slaves be sent into slavery, but decided to purchase the claims of all others.

The Indian Springs treaty of 1821 was negotiated by Georgia slave-holders. When they made the population of Black Seminoles slaves of the United States, there was no apparent desire to free the Black Seminoles from the slave industry. Jesup indicated in his report to the Senate that, as field commander and chief, he felt that having the Army take custody of the blacks and then paying off claimants was the best military policy. It seems probable that Van Buren and Secretary of War Poinsett applied this policy modification only to this single case, but Jesup knew that the modification must prevail to end the war.

Just before the court of inquiry of 1836, Congressman John Quincy Adams generally endorsed a similar policy in connection with the war. Adams responded to critics who declared that the federal government had no right to interfere with slavery. He noted that during the Revolution and the War of 1812, it was the federal government that interceded on behalf of the slave industry to make claims for slaves in the peace treaties with England. Adams declared:

> But the war power of Congress over the institution of slavery in the States is yet far more extensive. Suppose the case of a servile war, complicated, as to some extent it is even now, with an Indian war; suppose Congress were called to raise armies, to supply money from the whole union, to suppress a servile insurrection, would they have no authority to interfere with the institution of slavery? The issue of a servile war may be disastrous. By war the slave may emancipate himself; it may become necessary for the master to recognize his emancipation by a treaty of peace.... It would be equivalent to saying that Congress have no constitutional authority to make peace.... They must and will interfere with it—perhaps to sustain it by war; perhaps to abolish it with peace.[61]

Adams expounded a constitutional theory that had been applied in previous wars with a foreign power. The notion that slaves could be liberated to achieve peace directly applied to the Seminole War and to terms solicited by Abraham. Adams's concept of war powers was far-reaching. He theorized that under war powers slaves *can* be liberated, not that they *must* be. However, his ideas were rebuked by a Congress in which the slave industry was dominant. Though the idea might have been helpful to MLR, it also might have been used to demand enslavement; or if necessary, the contingencies of war and war powers could have demanded a policy of enslavement for all blacks and Indians in the United States. However, Adams could not execute his view of war powers from his seat in Congress. In Washington, the slave industry was dominant.

In battle, MLR had a forceful voice that initiated policy by its very success. Military realities had made a quasi-legislature of the battle-field. Adams spoke of war powers in the hands of the executive and legislative branches, but battlefield contingencies had forced the com-mander in the field to co-opt executive power and make policy in the field—granting liberty, an act that could not have been accomplished in Washington in 1838.

When Abraham and 90 other Black Seminoles arrived in New Orleans along with Native Seminoles, a lawyer representing an individual slaveholder immediately got a court order to claim all 90 blacks as the slaveholder's property. General Gaines, the commander of the Western Military District of the United States, had been fighting the Black Seminoles since he had ordered Colonel Clinch to destroy the Negro fort in 1816. General Gaines had been pinned down and nearly starved by Abraham and other Seminoles in 1836. But now Gaines ignored orders from the commissioner of Indian affairs to deliver the blacks back into slavery. Gaines resisted the court order and the demands of the New Orleans sheriff. He also went into court and argued that the blacks were not, nor had ever been, slaves of any whites; that they were all—men, women, and children—prisoners of war under the authority of the president only.

The judge rejected Gaines's argument, saying it was better to remove such formidable foes from the hands of potential savage enemies in Arkansas. Nevertheless, Gaines, who conducted this defense out of his own resources, appealed to a higher court, at which time the slaveholder dropped the case. All the Black Seminoles were sent on to Arkansas.[62]

The same lawyer for the claimant pursued the 90 blacks to Arkansas and made the same appeal to Acting Governor Samuel Roane and to General Mathew Arbuckle, commander of Fort Gibson. He laid claim to the blacks in the name of the commissioner of Indian affairs. The gover-nor and the general both turned him down on the grounds of public safe-ty. Neither man wanted the Seminole War to erupt in peaceful Arkansas.[63]

By May 1838, Jesup had retired and General Zachary Taylor was in command of U.S. forces in Florida. Taylor made a zealous effort to move all Seminoles west, but he made it known to his superiors that he would not execute the Treaty of Payne's Landing. From the beginning of his tenure as field commander, Taylor had treated all blacks whom he captured or who surrendered under the Articles of Capitulation as prisoners of war; then all were sent to Arkansas.[64] When the War Department ordered him to assist in obtaining the 90 Black Seminoles in the company of Abraham, Taylor said the following: "I know nothing of the Negroes in question, nor of the subject, further than what is contained in the communication above referred to; but I must state distinctly for the information of all concerned, that, while I shall hold myself ever ready to do the utmost in my power to get the Indians and their Negroes out of Florida, as well as to remove them to their new homes west of the Mississippi, I cannot for a moment consent to meddle with this transaction, as to be concerned for the benefit of Collins, the Creek Indians, or any one else."[65]

According to Congressman Joshua Giddings, this language from a brigadier general to the secretary of war was "received at the War Department without reproof." After Jesup's retirement, it seems that the Articles of Capitulation negotiated by Abraham and the Seminole chiefs had, to a very great extent, become the de facto law of the land. This fact is underscored by the actions of Gaines, Governor Roane, General Arbuckle, and Taylor. Finally, the slave industry pressured its legislators in Washington to take up the matter with the War Department. Secretary Poinsett, through the commissioner of Indian affairs, declared that "the Government held the power and constitutional right to dispose of prisoners of war, whatever their character may be."[66]

The original goal of the Seminoles, like that of all of the Indians, was to remain in their homelands east of the Mississippi. Most knew that they had no realistic chance to remain. As it became apparent that the Articles of Capitulation were being executed, the number of Seminole resisters began to dwindle. Nevertheless, there were holdouts who either did not trust the articles or simply wanted to remain in their ancestral homes. Those Seminoles who surrendered or were captured, black or native, were sent west by General Taylor as prisoners of war.

The few remaining Seminoles kept the U.S. Army at full troop strength.[67] In spite of this fact, before his retirement from Florida, Taylor had made tentative plans to divide Florida into districts of 20 square miles each. Each district would have contained 40 soldiers and 5 topographical engineers. This plan would have required a troop strength of 30,000 to 40,000 men. Taylor retired from Florida in April 1840. In his report to Congress, he stated, "[T]he enemy in several instances had been found, chased, and some killed, but they were far from being caught or subdued." [68]

General Walker Armistead took command until May 1841. Like Taylor, he came no closer to military success, and he continued to send Black and Native Seminoles to Arkansas. Following Armistead, Colonel William Worth became the Florida commander. Worth's command followed the same military pattern, in spite of new tactics. U.S. forces normally did not attempt to fight between May and October or November because of the threat of disease; however, Worth attempted summer campaigns in an effort to interrupt the Seminole growing seasons.

In July and August 1841, Worth reported 60 soldiers dead from illness and 5,000 men having reported to sickbay. In spite of his efforts, the Seminoles were not yet conquered. Their population had been greatly reduced, but hostile Seminoles remained, continuing to inflict surprise attacks on troops and settlers. Worth continued to send Seminoles to Arkansas.

By May 1842, President John Tyler had instructed Worth to end the war. Tyler estimated that no more than 240 Seminoles remained, with perhaps 80 warriors. He noted that it was impossible to catch those remaining and too expensive to maintain the full troop strength. Tyler said that the Florida settlers would have to be armed to protect themselves. [69] Hostilities with the Seminoles continued until 1858, but the Articles of Capitulation proved to be the most effective factor in the process that led to political and military solutions. [70]

Jesup had engineered the key military solution by providing the blacks with freedom in the west; but the political pressure in Washington had originated with the constituent slaveholders. Before leaving office, Secretary of War Poinsett instructed General Armistead to once again attempt to end the war under the terms of "Payne's Landing and by the interest and feelings of the people of Florida." [71]

The interests of the people of Florida were primarily their claims on the remaining Black Seminoles. This fact, coupled with lingering apprehensions about the Black Seminoles, had been the primary cause for war. Jesup had paid the claims of the Creeks to keep Abraham and others moving to Arkansas. In 1841, abolitionist Congressman Giddings noted: "Money was now offered certain influential men of the Seminole and Exiles [blacks] to induce them to exert their influence with their friends to emigrate.... It was therefore proposed that Congress should make an appropriation for the purpose of purchasing such Exiles; yet the bill making it was general in its provisions.... This money was to be expended to purchase the pretended interest of certain white men to the individual Exiles whom they claimed as property." [72]

Apparently, it was hoped that the resources expended would remove all obstacles for the parties concerned. This tactic had been used earlier by Jesup. The purposes of the expenditures were disguised in Congress; they were voted on and passed by Congress as two separate bills for a total of $1.1 million. [73]

Later, in 1842, Congress requested a report from President Tyler on the disposition of slaves captured in the war. In the report, Secretary of War George Crawford listed 78 captured slaves, but he denied having any knowledge of, or means to gain knowledge of, any payment for those slaves. By this covert means, it appears that the dominant factors that caused the war to begin and continue were satisfied. [74]

In Crawford's report it was stated that Captain John T. Sprague had helped deliver Seminoles from Florida to Arkansas. Sprague had been in the war since 1835. Concerning the war's conclusion, Sprague wrote:

> With the surrender of Indians in Florida, and their embarkation for Arkansas, an important question arose in relation to Negroes in their possession. . . . The independence and freedom so long enjoyed, unchecked, had unfitted him for any usefulness to the claimant. . . . These Negroes had learned to speak the Indian language, together with a knowledge of English, and intimacy with the habits of whites, soon gave them an ascendancy, when the slave becomes the master. The Negroes from the commencement of the Florida war, have, for their numbers, been the most formidable foe, more blood thirsty, active, and revengeful, than the Indians. . . . The lives of citizens and their property, demanded that they should be sent far beyond the country with which they were familiar. . . . The swamps and hammocks of Florida could, for years, be made safe retreats from bondage, where without labor or expense, they might defy the efforts of armed men. . . . Ten resolute Negroes, with a knowledge of the country, are sufficient to desolate the frontier, from one extent to the other. To obviate all difficulty, the claimant of the Negro in possession of the Indian, was, upon identifying and proving property, paid a fair equivalent, determined by a board of officers. [75]

Captain Sprague, who sailed from Tampa Bay to New Orleans, steamed up the Mississippi and then traveled in wagons with the Seminoles to Arkansas. Perhaps it is not inconceivable that a military officer with these experiences would have knowledge about appropriations and expenditures to the slave industry, that the War Department lacked. It is probable that northern congressmen and their constituents would never have favored such expenditures if they knew the relationship to slavery. If the expenditures had not been forthcoming, however, it is conceivable that the "Great Seminole War" would have extended into the Civil War and that northerners would have been the allies of MLR. After traversing the Florida theater for more than a decade, Sprague indicated that the primary concern was that Spain or England would further arm the blacks and bring in more black troops from the West Indies, causing a general slave uprising. Although he was from Michigan, he did not believe this to be an issue that could be "sheltered" in philanthropy; it had to be addressed by North and South "in the forum or in the field." [76]

Sprague addressed a consistent theme in American politics—an apprehension with Florida. Fears of slave rebellions had been expressed since the days of the Continental Congress. Though the Second Seminole War had been foretold by Jefferson and Jackson, the scope and dimension of the conflict were probably unpredictable. During the Patriots War, Georgia Governor Mitchell expressed concern over a general African slave rebellion, centered in Florida, with help provided from the West Indies. But in essence Sprague's comments perhaps underscore the universal plight of enslaved peoples. Given a reasonable opportunity of success, blacks would champion the cause of personal and group freedom.

The Treaty of Fort Moultrie identified the Seminoles as a people separate from the Creeks, but it continued to deny that Black Seminoles were anything except property. They were only pawns of negotiation by third parties. This interpretation begs the question: Did Black Seminoles seek the status of slaves for legal and diplomatic protection?

In the Second Seminole War approximately 1,500 U.S. soldiers were killed. The federal government spent approximately $40 million on the war. Giddings estimated that 300 to 500 mostly noncombatants were captured, that the federal government had spent $80,000 per slave captured, and that three white soldiers had died to enslave each African. [77]

Notes

1. Giddings, *Exiles*, 173.
2. Sprague, *Origin*, 21.
3. Giddings, *Exiles*, 78–81.
4. Andrew Jackson, *Correspondence of Andrew Jackson*, vol. 5, ed. John Spencer Bassett, (Washington, D.C.: Carnegie Institution, 1928), 132.

5. Monroe, *Writings*, 88.

6. Edward Ressen, *Jacksonian America*, rev. ed. (Urbana, Ill.: University of Illinois Press, 1985), 296–99; Peters, *Florida Wars*, 87.

7. Sprague, *Origin*, 75.

8. Ibid., 80–90; Mulroy, *Border*, 28–32.

9. *Am. St. P.*, 5, *Military Affairs*, 6:68–69, 454, 458.

10. Ibid., 454.

11. *Am. St. P.*, 2, *Indian Affairs*, 2:411, 414.

12. *Am. St. P.*, 2, *Military Affairs*, 6:458.

13. Porter, *Negro*, 305–8.

14. *Am. St. P.*, 5, *Military Affairs*, 7:852.

15. Giddings, *Exiles*, 84–87; Sprague, *Origin*, 72.

16. Sprague, *Origin*, 74.

17. *Am. St. P.*, 5, *Military Affairs*, 6:56–59, 465; Giddings, *Exiles*, 90–91.

18. *Am. St. P.*, 5, *Military Affairs*, 6:56–58.

19. Porter, *Negro*, 311–12.

20. Ibid., 312–14; Giddings, *Exiles*, 99–106; M. M. Cohen, *Notices of Florida* (1836; reprint, Gainesville, Fla.: University Press of Florida, 1964), 67–79.

21. Cohen, *Notices*, 67–79; Peters, *Florida Wars*, 107; Giddings, *Exiles*, 99–100.

22. Porter, *Negro*, 314.

23. *Am. St. P.*, 5, *Military Affairs*, 6:19, 20.

24. Sprague, *Origin*, 110–11; Giddings, *Exiles*, 118–24; Cohen, *Notices*, 83–103; Porter, *Negro*, 315–16.

25. *Am. St. P.*, 5, *Military Affairs*, 7:296.

26. Sprague, *Origin*, 114.

27. *Am. St. P.*, 5, *Military Affairs*, 7:125.

28. Jackson, *Correspondence*, vol. 5, 419.

29. *Am. St. P.*, 5, *Military Affairs*, 7:135.

30. Ibid., 139.

31. Ibid., 143.

32. Ibid., 149–50.

33. Clausewitz, *On War*, 23.

34. Sprague, *Origin*, 131.

35. Ibid., 132.

36. Ibid.

37. Ibid., 143.

38. *Am. St. P.*, 5, *Military Affairs*, 7:159.

39. Ibid., 820–21.

40. Jackson, *Correspondence*, vol. 5, 434.

41. *Am. St. P.*, 5, *Military Affairs*, 7:832–34.

42. Ibid.

43. Giddings, *Exiles*, 139–50; Sprague, *Origin*, 177–81.

44. *Am. St. P.*, 5, *Military Affairs*, 7:835.

45. Giddings, *Exiles*, 144–48; *Am. St. P.*, 5, *Military Affairs*, 7:838.

46. *Am. St. P.*, 5, *Military Affairs*, 7:838–39.

47. Sprague, *Origin*, 173.

48. *Am. St. P.*, 5, *Military Affairs*, 7:876.

49. Giddings, *Exiles*, 271.

50. *Congressional Information Service*, General Jesup's report to the Senate after retiring from command, 25th Cong., 2d sess., 1838, S. Doc. 507, 2–12.

51. Porter, *Negro*, 317–21; Giddings, *Exiles*, 139–60; Covington, *Seminoles of Florida*, 85–95.

52. Porter, *Negro*, 320.

53. *Am. St. P.*, 5, *Military Affairs*, 7:872.

54. Sprague, *Origin*, 208–26.

55. Giddings, *Exiles*, 181–90.

56. Sprague, *Origin*, 200–201.

57. Ibid., 201–2.

58. U.S. Senate, 25th Cong., 2d sess., 1842, S. Doc. 507, 9–10.

59. Porter, *Negro*, 332.

60. Giddings, *Exiles*, 158–62.

61. *Congressional Globe*, 24th Cong., 2d sess., 1836, 4040–47.

62. Giddings, *Exiles*, 209–11.

63. Ibid.

64. Ibid., 224–26.

65. Ibid., 226.

66. Ibid., 227.

67. Sprague, *Origin*, 263.

68. Ibid., 221, 227.

69. Ibid., 243, 247, 261–70, 475.

70. Peters, *Florida Wars*, 267.

71. Giddings, *Exiles*, 280.

72. Ibid., 280–81; *Congressional Globe*, 27th Cong., lst sess., 1841, appendix, 6.

73. Sprague, *Origin*, 250; Giddings, *Exiles*, 281–82.

74. *Congressional Globe*, 27th Cong., 2d sess., 1842, H. Doc. 55, 1–9.

75. Sprague, *Origin*, 309–10.

76. Ibid., 310.

77. Giddings, *Exiles*, 310–16.

Chapter 8

The Indirect Impact of MLR

During the Second Seminole War, macro-level rebellion MLR was a political force that altered federal policy. This effect can be directly observed in the Articles of Capitulation, which emerged from the battlefield. Additionally, MLR was an indirect factor in the failure of President Van Buren to be reelected and in the repeal of the congressional gag rule. The repeal of the gag rule was important because the gag rule was a legislative barrier that had prevented northern and southern congressmen from engaging in the fatal debates that helped bring on the Civil War. Therefore, macro-rebellion can be seen not only as a coconspirator of congressional abolitionists, but also as a catalyst of the Civil War. U.S. politicians in the federal government had been responding to the presence of Black Seminoles since John Jay and the Continental Congress sought to convince Spain to repeal the Edict of 1693. This effort was begun by Jay and completed by the Washington administration. It cannot be said, though, that these diplomatic efforts of Washington and Jay initiated U.S. knowledge of the Black Seminoles. During the previous centuries, American colonists had become acquainted with the rebels.

Washington's urgent efforts to repeal the edict demonstrate U.S. awareness of and concern with the Black Seminole threat to the slave industry. Georgia's documented claims on Black Seminoles extend from the days of James Oglethorpe to those of John Jay and George

Washington. The continuity of claims and knowledge of the Black Seminole impact on growth and development made the edict an obvious target. However, this long and unbroken trail of events also clearly indicates that the threat to the slave industry was facilitated by Spain. Between the repeal of the edict and the Articles of Capitulation, the primary U.S. initiatives concerning the Black Seminoles dealt with third parties. The treaty of 1795 stipulated that Spain would capture and return slaves. All treaties with the Creeks had these same stipulations. The Creeks had worked with the British and then with the Americans for more than a century as slave catchers. The Treaties of Colerain and New York were key treaties in which Creeks promised the return of slaves. The Seminoles were viewed as a part of the Creek nation, but the Treaty of Fort Moultrie legally established the Seminoles as sovereign in the eyes of U.S. policymakers.

The Treaty of Payne's Landing in 1832 continued to view the Black Seminoles as pawns in the hands of third parties. In the process of negotiating this treaty and in the Seminole response to it, Abraham assumed a dominant role. He was certainly the most prominent Black Seminole and perhaps the most dominant of all Seminoles. This conclusion would seem to be a logical one. The Seminole Indian commissioner, Penieres, informed Governor Jackson 14 years before the commencement of the Second Seminole War that the blacks were the rulers of the Seminoles, in spite of their being technically classified as slaves. Governor Jackson relayed this intelligence to the War Department and warned that the Black Seminoles must be removed or, "scenes of murder and confusion will exist, and lead to unhappy consequences which cannot be controlled."[1] Indian agent Thompson and Florida Governor Duval made the same conclusions 14 years later, stating that the Black Seminoles would dictate war and peace for the Seminoles. Additionally, in documents transferred from the War Department to Congress, General Jesup informed policymakers that the Second Seminole War was a "Negro war" rather than an Indian war. Therefore, Abraham can rightfully be viewed as the most influential of the Seminole leaders.

The commencement of the Second Seminole War during the presidency of Andrew Jackson underscored the prophecy of peril he made while he was Florida's first governor. Abraham was the primary interpreter and diplomat of the Seminoles. In this capacity, he appears to have been the architect of their policy, rejecting removal unless blacks were given free passage to Arkansas. Also, he most likely initiated the strategy of waging a protracted war to achieve these terms.

General Scott was ordered to remove the Indians to Arkansas and return the blacks to slavery. Those orders led to war. Clausewitz states that war is only an extension of politics. Consequently, the battlefield is a political arena or quasi legislature that is capable of initiating policies. In Congress, Parliament, or other variants in republican government, policy is influenced by a number of factors, such as money, votes, or reason. In the battlefield, the throes of war can become the primary determinant of policy.

Correspondence from the battlefield indicates that the Seminoles conducted an inscrutable guerrilla campaign for at least five years. Within this context, Abraham and Jesup initiated peace talks. In the Articles of Capitulation, the Treaty of Payne's Landing was enforced with one key modification: Black Seminoles, deemed as bona fide Seminole property, were permitted to emigrate. Ultimately, Jesup modified U.S. policy objectives to the point that he advocated the key Seminole policy goals. The success of the Seminoles is measured in the general execution of their policy objective. They did not defeat the United States, but they did prohibit U.S. commanders from executing their orders.

The United States sought the unification of master and slave; the Seminoles sought the separation of master and slave. The Articles of Capitulation codified these conflicting objectives, and Jesup eventually began to compensate those parties that claimed to have been separated from their slaves.

Jesup believed that U.S. troops could pursue the Seminoles throughout Florida for an indefinite number of years without achieving the stated policy goals. In conceding to the articles, he accepted terms that Abraham and other Seminoles had been seeking since the Treaty of Payne's Landing. Therefore, from the battlefield, the policies of MLR emanated to Jesup as if from a quasi legislature. He and other generals executed these policies. The policy of freedom for the slaves originated with the slaves themselves. Eventually, with all commanders executing the policy, the goals of the War Department were superseded. Finally, the executive branch, Congress, and southern proprietors in the slave industry accepted the policy of MLR that had been crafted exclusively through a successful guerrilla campaign (see figures C and D on pages 74 and 125).

U.S. objectives for the Seminole War changed as a direct result of MLR. Presidents Jackson and Van Buren, in response to the slave industry, ordered commanders, through the War Department, to enforce the Payne's Landing treaty. Battlefield stalemates, however, converted commanders into agents for MLR. To this extent, the chain of command was subverted. For four years, Van Buren presided over a failing policy. The policy was changed by the opposing end of the command structure, and the slave holders, who had demanded the Black Seminoles as property, were compensated. Under such circumstances, it was perhaps impossible for Van Buren to remain unscathed by that policy. In 1840, Martin Van Buren ran for reelection. Regarding the campaign, Giddings makes these comments:

> The Presidential election of this year was conducted differently from any that had preceded it. The opponents of Mr. Van Buren arraigned him before the people for his extravagance in the expenditure of public treasure... Among the subjects made prominent before the country, was that of the extravagant expenditures in prosecuting the Florida War. Speeches were made in Congress exposing the various practices by which the people's money was squandered in that unfortunate conflict...These speeches were printed in pamphlet form and sent to the people in vast numbers; but the real cause of the war, the deep depravity of that policy which sought the enslavement of the Exiles, was not mentioned; nor does it appear that any member of Congress was conscious, even, that such a people as the Exiles was living in Florida. But nevertheless, it is quite certain that this war proved one of the principle causes of Mr. Van Buren's defeat.[2]

In *Martin Van Buren and the American Political System*, Donald B. Cole writes that by the spring of 1840, as the presidential campaign was in progress, a principal burden was the Seminole War. The Democrats and Whigs debated over expenditures for the war. This debate caused a great deal of hostility to be directed toward Van Buren.[3] It seems that other campaign issues weakened his candidacy, and the war was an added burden that helped ensure his defeat.[4]

For four years, Van Buren ordered the execution of the Payne's Landing treaty. The battlefield became the first casualty of this impossible policy due to its failure to serve as a vehicle of enforcement. General Scott was relieved of his command in Florida even before Van Buren's presidency because he could not enforce the treaty. Scott was a victim of President Jackson's high expectations for a "ten-day" victory. In four years, after millions of dollars had been spent and more than 1,000 were dead, stalemate reverberated from the battlefield to the White House, giving voters one more reason to reject Van Buren.

Van Buren's loss of the presidency was not a direct result of MLR, but MLR helped to shape his fate. For four years, MLR was directly opposed to his objective. In all probability, any aspect of U.S. politics that depended on the fulfillment of the Payne's Landing treaty was forced to adjust to the new policy. Conversely, there were entities that were akin to the goals of MLR. At the core of the Seminole War was the resistance to slavery. In the 1830s, a national abolitionist movement was inaugurated. Abolitionist Congressman Joshua Giddings indicates that the national movement, including members in Congress, was unaware of the fight against slavery being waged in Florida. In general, though, the Seminoles and the abolitionists had a common objective in opposing slavery.

By 1832, northern abolitionists were alarmed over many aspects of slavery and sought to influence changes in national policies concerning slaves by petitioning Congress. But in 1835, a southern-dominated Congress passed a resolution that prevented discussion of such abolitionist petitions. The South reasoned that the Constitution forbade any federal interference with the institution of slavery in the various states; additionally, they said the petitions were disruptive and could lead to disunion. This 1835 resolution became known as the "gag rule."[5]

Because the gag rule prevented all discussion of slavery, abolitionists in Congress often went to great lengths to connect other issues to slavery in the remotest sense. Sometimes this method allowed them to engage in limited discourses on slavery before being called to order by southern congressmen. However, the continuation of the Seminole War required annual appropriations from Congress, and the president had to keep Congress informed about the war's progress. Therefore, with the enslavement of the Seminole rebels being the core issue of the war, abolitionists were provided a means of transcending the gag rule. Eventually, by 1844, the Seminole War issue helped them vote out the rule.

In 1836, some congressmen from Alabama sought relief for their constituents who were made refugees by efforts to move Creeks to the West. John Quincy Adams took advantage of this occasion to discuss a similar resolution that had been approved for refugees in Florida. He argued that in both instances the citizens were covered by the war powers of Congress and the president, which, he said, incorporated vast indefinite authority unstipulated by the Constitution. Adams infuriated southern congressmen by saying that war powers gave authority to do anything, from providing for refugees to separating slaves from their masters. He argued that during servile wars, such as the wars in Florida, if liberating slaves was in the best interests of the nation, then the federal government was required to do so.[6]

Unlike the petitions concerning slavery that were pouring into Congress, the Seminole War demanded discussion. As Adams spoke in

1836, President Jackson and Congress were proceeding with the court of inquiry examining General Scott's conduct. Even if southern legislators sought to direct discussion away from the Black Seminoles, the very nature of the war provided a legitimate issue related to slavery that congressional abolitionists could use to evade the gag rule and chastise the institution.

In 1841, southern congressmen proposed the first of two resolutions that provided $1.1 million to assist in the removal of the Seminoles. They had just narrowly defeated a proposal by John Quincy Adams to repeal the gag rule. Adams, Giddings, and other congressional abolitionists were using every opportunity to challenge the rule.[7] With this proposal, Congressman Giddings first acquired proof that the principal issue of the war was slavery. He decided to use this aspect of the war to test and weaken the gag rule. Speaking to the whole House, Giddings commented:

> I am somewhat incredulous as to its [the war's] immediate termination by the means presented by the gentleman from South Carolina. In order that our legislature shall conduce to its early close, we must act with reference to the causes which have unfortunately involved us in hostilities. This war has occupied the attention of the Executive for the last five years; our whole military force has been employed to carry it forward; our officers and soldiers have fallen victims to the climate; our funds have been squandered; but the propriety of this vast expenditure of life and treasure have been kept from the public view.... No member has attempted to explain the causes of its commencement.[8]

Giddings explained as much of the Seminole history as he knew at that time. In this explanation, he pointed out how blacks had become the key point of contention between U.S. slaveholders and both Indians and Spaniards. Then he presented documentation from the War Department that proved that the effort to enslave the Black Seminoles was the cause of the war. Giddings expressed shock at the suggestion that a resolution calling for additional expenditures could now suddenly bring an end to the war. Southern members of Congress insisted that the gag rule prohibited exposure of the war's relationship to slavery, but the presiding officer, Nathan Clifford of Maine, allowed Giddings to continue.[9]

Giddings said:

> I regard this interposition of the federal power to sustain slavery as unwarranted by the Constitution. This war is, therefore, unconstitutional, unjust, and an outrage upon the rights of the people of the free

states. . . . I hold that if the slaves of Georgia or of any other state leave their masters and go among the Indians, the federal government has no right, no constitutional power to employ the army for their recapture, or to expend the national treasure to purchase them from the Indians. . . . These extraordinary efforts of the President to sustain slavery, will constitute an interesting chapter in our political history. . . . They have been kept from the people, and my present object is to bring them forth to the public gaze. . . . And, Sir, our army was put in motion to capture Blacks and slaves. Our officers and soldiers became slave-catchers, companions of the most degraded class of human beings who disgrace that slave-cursed region. . . . Indeed, it seems to have been an object with some of the officers employed in Florida to induce government itself to enter into the business of capturing and selling slaves.[10]

While Giddings spoke, southern members screamed for him to be silenced. But he was quickly able to show the ties to new appropriations requested. Southerners gathered around him in an effort to intimidate him. Giddings received a continuous stream of attacks from the South, including one suggestion that he be lynched, and he traded death threats with another member. Julius Alford of Georgia ran to attack Giddings but was restrained. In his inaugural address, President William Henry Harrison alluded to Giddings as he denounced those who would bring on a civil war.[11] Giddings's three-hour speech was perhaps the most deadly blow that had been struck against the gag rule and, therefore, against slavery, which had become a national issue in the 1830s.[12]

The abolitionist movement against slavery was carried on through the underground railroad and by other means. Nevertheless, the gag rule's prohibition against all speeches and petitions further strengthened the South and weakened the abolitionists.

In Congress, the Seminole War was an issue that ensnared the South in a web of its own lies. The South's insistence that the war had nothing to do with slavery permitted the most volatile of all slave issues to transcend the carefully crafted gag rule. Giddings's speech was distributed nationwide. Had the Seminole War been put down in "ten days," as Jackson had hoped, there may not have been a comparable means by which to transcend U.S. law and thereby strike blows for the abolition of slavery.

In 1842, John Quincy Adams presented a petition from 46 of his constituents requesting a peaceful dissolving of the Union because of southern outrages such as the gag rule. Several southern congressmen wanted to censure Adams, and they charged him with and tried him for treason. Among the issues that caused extreme anger in the trial was Adams's enunciation that slaves could be freed under war powers. The Seminole War brought this policy to reality and clearly demonstrated its validity and practicality. In this instance, the Black Seminoles' struggle played an indirect role in the South's unsuccessful effort to censure Adams, moving the nation closer to repeal of the gag rule.[13]

Adams, Giddings, and other abolitionist congressmen used numerous issues concerning slavery to oppose the gag rule, but few of these issues actually provided opportunities for legitimate debate. One such issue involved the slave ship *Creole*. The *Creole* was loaded with Virginia slaves headed for New Orleans. En route, the slaves revolted and sailed into the Bahamas. The British freed the slaves, but the southern legislators demanded their return.[14] Giddings was poised to use the introduction of resolutions on the *Creole* case to challenge the gag rule, but the Southerners refused to act.[15] They realized that the abolitionists were eager to overturn the rule.

Giddings argued that the federal government had no jurisdiction over slavery—that only state government did. Therefore, he said, neither state nor federal government had jurisdiction when the *Creole* revolt occurred in international waters. The British, then, returned to the slaves their God-given natural rights of freedom.[16]

Before Giddings could state his case, southern congressmen attacked him and had him called to order for breaching the gag rule. Giddings was censured and removed from his House seat.[17] The resolution that removed Giddings stated:

> Whereas the Hon. Joshua R. Giddings has this day presented to this House a series of resolutions touching the most important interest connected with a large portion of the Union, now a subject of negotiation between the United States and Great Britain of the most delicate nature, the results of which may eventually involve those nations and perhaps the whole civilized world in war; and whereas it is the duty of every good citizen, and particularly the duty of every selected agent and representative of the people, to discountenance all efforts to create excitement, dissatisfaction, and division among the people of the United States.... [T]herefore, Resolved, that this House hold the conduct of the said member as altogether unwarranted ... deserving the severe condemnation of the people of this country, and of this body in particular.[18]

In general, the petitions that flooded Congress calling for abolition came from the constituents of Giddings, Adams, and most of the other northern congressmen. When southern congressmen effected the removal of one of the North's leading representatives it was like tossing the gauntlet to the abolitionists. Giddings's removal was a challenge that forced the abolitionists to organize as no previous event had, either nationwide or in Congress. Not only did the abolitionists determine to overthrow the gag rule, which Giddings was challenging, but they were preparing to overthrow the slave industry that had dominated national politics since the Washington administration. The Seminole rebels would prove to be an immovable source of strength in this challenge.[19]

In spite of threats of lynching from southern congressmen, Giddings made his way back to Ohio and prepared for reelection. He was reelected by a 7,469-to-393 vote in May 1842. His constituents demanded that he reintroduce the Creole resolutions. Even southern members acknowledged that Giddings's return was a great triumph for abolitionists. Giddings presented the Creole resolutions despite a few protesters, but no member attempted to invoke the gag rule.[20] According to Stewart, "Through the process of his censure, re-election, and reassertion of the Creole resolutions, Giddings had successfully defied his party and nearly all of Congress. The continued independence of the antislavery Whigs was now insured. Congress would henceforth be unable to escape sectional issues by forcing the agitators out."[21]

Giddings's presentation of the Creole resolutions unofficially ended the gag rule; it was officially voted down by Congress in February 1844. Before that vote, Giddings made many comments on the rule. He said that Adams had sought disunion because of the rule's unfairness to the North, and he agreed that the rule challenged the permanency of the Union. He reminded members that the Articles of Confederation gave each state sole authority over its slaves and that the Constitution did not touch on the issue. But he again concurred with Adams that war powers permitted federal interference with the institution. He stated, "It is, I believe, well understood by military men; it was practiced by General Jackson, General Gaines, and General Jesup, and I believe by General Scott, while commanding our armies in the South. They did not hesitate to severe the relation of master and slave whenever they believed the public good demanded it."[22]

Giddings commented on the South's unwillingness to tolerate federal interference under the war powers, but he noted its demands for federal military interference in support of the slave industry. He spoke of the case of the Negro fort, in which "270 men, women, and children were instantaneously murdered, for no other crime than a love of liberty."[23] Giddings pointed to the millions of federal dollars expended by southern-dominated administrations: "For the purpose of enabling the owners of southern slaves to regain their runaway Blacks, we waged a bloody and expensive war with the Indians of Florida."[24]

Giddings and other abolitionists had succeeded in undermining the gag rule in 1842 and they voted it out in 1844. Even while the rule existed, violent threats had been uttered in Congress, but after the legislative barrier was removed, heated debates occurred that hastened the commencement of the Civil War. From this perspective, the rebels can be seen to have contributed indirectly to the abolition of slavery in the United States.

Notes

1. *Am. St. P.*, 2, *Indian Affairs*, 2:414.

2. Giddings, *Exiles*, 274–75.

3. Donald B. Cole, *Martin Van Buren and the American Political System* (Princeton, N.J.: Princeton University Press, 1984), 366.

4. Edward M. Shepherd, *American Statesman* (Boston and New York: Houghton, Mifflin and Co., 1899), 365–66; Dennis Tilden Lynch, *An Epoch and a Man* (New York: Horace Liveright, 1929), 452.

5. Joshua R. Giddings, *Speeches in Congress* (Cleveland, Ohio: John P. Jewett and Co., 1853), 52.

6. *Congressional Globe*, 24th Cong., 2d sess., 1836, 4037–50.

7. James Brewer Stewart, *Joshua R. Giddings and the Tactics of Radical Politics* (Cleveland, Ohio: Case Western Reserve University Press, 1970), 62–63.

8. Giddings, *Speeches*, 1–2.

9. Giddings, *Exiles*, 280–81.

10. Giddings, *Speeches*, 6–12.

11. Stewart, *Joshua R. Giddings*, 65–62.

12. James M. McPherson, "The Fight against the Gag Rule: Joshua Leavitt and Antislavery Insurgency in the Whig Party, 1839–42," *Journal of Negro History* 48 (1963): 177–95.

13. John Quincy Adams, *The Diary of John Quincy Adams, 1794–1845* (New York: Charles Scribner's Sons, 1951), 533–35; Joshua R. Giddings, *History of the Rebellion: Its Authors and Causes* (Cleveland, Ohio: Follet, Foster and Co., 1864), 160–72; Stewart, *Joshua R. Giddings*, 71–72.

14. McPherson, "Fight against the Gag Rule," 188.

15. Ibid., 193; Stewart, *Joshua R. Giddings*, 73.

16. Stewart, *Joshua R. Giddings*, 70; McPherson, "Fight against the Gag Rule," 188.

17. *Congressional Globe*, 27th Cong., 2d sess., 1842, 346.

18. Ibid.

19. Stewart, *Joshua R. Giddings*, 75–76.

20. Ibid., 77.

21. Ibid.

22. Giddings, *Speeches*, 55.

23. Ibid., 59.

24. Ibid., 58.

Bibliography

Primary Sources

Adams, John Quincy. *The Diary of John Quincy Adams, 1794–1845.* New York: Charles Scribner's Sons, 1951.

———. *Memoirs of John Quincy Adams.* Vol. 4. Ed. Charles Francis Adams. Philadelphia: J. B. Lippincott and Co., 1875.

Bartram, William. *Travels.* 1792. Reprint, Savannah, Ga.: Beehive Press, 1973.

Brevard, Caroline Mays. *A History of Florida.* Deland, Fla.: Florida Historical Society, 1924.

Britton, Wiley. *Memoirs of the Rebellion on the Border, 1863.* Chicago: Cushing, Thomas, 1882.

Calhoun, John C. *The Papers of John C. Calhoun.* Vol. 2, 1817–1818. Ed. W. Edwin Hemphill. Columbia, S.C.: University of South Carolina Press, 1963.

———. *The Papers of John C. Calhoun.* Vol. 3, 1818–1819. Ed. W. Edwin Hemphill. Columbia, S.C.: University of South Carolina Press, 1967.

Clausewitz, Karl von. *On War.* Vol. 1. Trans. J. J. Graham. New York: Barnes and Noble, 1956.

Cohen, M. M. *Notices of Florida.* 1836. Reprint, Gainesville, Fla.: University Press of Florida, 1964.

Coleman, Kenneth. *Colonial Georgia.* New York: Charles Scribner's Sons, 1976.

Easterby, J. H., ed. *The Colonial Records of South Carolina: The Journal of the Commons House of Assembly.* Vol. 1, 1736–1739. Columbia, S.C.: Historical Commission of South Carolina, 1951.

———. *The Colonial Records of South Carolina: The Journal of the Commons House of Assembly.* Vol. 3, 1741–1742. Columbia, S.C.: Historical Commission of South Carolina, 1953.

——. *The Colonial Records of South Carolina: The Journal of the Commons House of Assembly.* Vol. 4, 1742–1744. Columbia, S.C.: Historical Commission of South Carolina, 1953.

Giddings, Joshua R. *Speeches in Congress.* Cleveland, Ohio: John P. Jewett and Co., 1853.

——. *The Exiles of Florida.* Columbus, Ohio: Follet, Foster and Co., 1858.

——. *History of the Rebellion: Its Authors and Causes.* Cleveland, Ohio: Follet, Foster and Co., 1864.

Glison, Rodney. *Journal of Army Life.* San Francisco: A. L. Bancroft and Co., 1874.

Hewatt, Alexander. *History of South Carolina and Georgia.* Vol. 1. London: Alexander Donaldson, 1779.

Hitchcock, Ethan Allen. *Fifty Years in Camp and Field: The Diary of Major General Ethan Allen Hitchcock.* Ed. W. A. Croffut. New York: G. P. Putnam's Sons, 1909.

Jackson, Andrew. *Correspondence of Andrew Jackson.* Vol. 5. Ed. John Spencer Bassett. Washington, D.C.: Carnegie Institution, 1928.

Jay, John. *The Correspondence and Public Papers of John Jay, 1782–1793.* Vol. 3. Ed. Henry P. Johnson. New York: J. P. Putnam's Sons, 1891.

Jefferson, Thomas. *The Papers of Thomas Jefferson.* Vols. 16, 17, and 20. Ed. Julian P. Boyd. Princeton, N.J.: Princeton University Press, 1961.

Jensen, Merrill, ed. *English Historical Documents to 1776.* New York: Oxford University Press, 1962.

Kent, R. K. "Palmares: An African State in Brazil." In *Maroon Societies: Rebel Slave Communities in the Americas.* Ed. Richard Price. Baltimore: Johns Hopkins University Press, 1979.

Madison, James. *The Papers of James Madison, 1787–1788.* Vol. 10. Ed. Robert A. Rutland. Chicago: University of Chicago Press, 1962.

——. *The Papers of James Madison, 1793–1795.* Vol. 15. Ed. Thomas A. Mason, Robert A. Rutland, Jeanne K. Sisson. Charlottesville, Va.: University Press of Virginia, 1985.

McCall, George A. *Letters from the Frontiers.* Philadelphia: J. B. Lippincott and Co., 1868.

Monroe, James. *The Writings of James Monroe, 1807–1816.* Vols. 5, 6, and 7. New York: AMS Press, 1969.

Oglethorpe, James E. *Some Account of the Design of the Trustees for Establishing Colonies in America.* 1732. Reprint, ed. Rodney M. Baine and Phinizy Spalding, Athens, Ga.: University of Georgia Press, 1990.

Perceval, John. "The Journal of the Earl of Egmont." In *The Colonial Records of Georgia*, vol. 5. Ed. Allen D. Candler. Atlanta: Franklin-Turner, 1906.

Ross, John. *The Papers of Chief John Ross, 1840–1866.* Vol. 2. Ed. Gary E. Moulton. Norman, Okla.: University of Oklahoma Press, 1984.

Salley, Alexander S. Jr., ed. *Narratives of Early Carolina, 1650–1708.* New York: Charles Scribner's Sons, 1910.

Siebert, Wilbur H. *Loyalist in East Florida.* Vols. 1 and 2. Deland, Fla.: Florida State Historical Society, 1929.

Sprague, John T. *The Origin, Progress, and Conclusion of the Florida War.* 1848. Reprint, Gainesville, Fla.: University Press of Florida, 1964.

Washington, George. *The Writings of George Washington.* Vol. 31, 1745–1799. Ed. John C. Fitzpatrick. Washington, D.C. U.S. Government Printing Office, 1936.

———. *The Papers of George Washington.* Presidential Series. Vol. 4. Ed. W. W. Abbott and Dorothy Twohig. Charlottesville, Va. and London: University Press of Virginia, 1993.

Secondary Sources

Abel, Annie H. *The American Indian as Slaveholder and Secessionist: An Omitted Chapter in the Diplomatic History of the Southern Confederacy.* Cleveland, Ohio: Arthur H. Clark, 1925.

Adams, Henry. *History of the United States of America.* Vol. 2. *During the First Administration of Thomas Jefferson.* New York: Charles Scribner's Sons, 1921.

———. *History of the United States of America.* Vol. 1. *During the Administration of Jefferson and Madison.* Englewood Cliffs, N.J.: Prentice-Hall, 1963.

———. *History of the United States, 1801–1809.* New York: Literary Classics of the United States, 1986.

Aptheker, Herbert. *American Negro Slave Revolts.* New York: Columbia University Press, 1943.

Bailey, Thomas A. *The American Pageant: A History of the Republic.* Boston: D. C. Heath and Co., 1966.

Barr, Alwyn. *Black Texans: A History of Negroes in Texas.* Austin, Tex.: Jenkins Publishing Co., 1973.

Beard, Charles and Mary. *The Beards' Basic History of the United States.* New York: Doubleday, Doran and Co., 1944.

———. *The Beards' New Basic History of the United States.* Revised by William Beard. Garden City, N.Y.: Doubleday and Co., 1968.

Blassingame, John W. *The Slave Community: Plantation Life in the Antebellum South.* Rev. and enl. ed. New York: Oxford University Press, 1979.

Bolt, Christine. *American Indian Policy and American Reform.* London: Allen and Unwin, 1987.

Bolton, Herbert E., and Mary Ross. *The Debatable Land.* Berkeley, Calif.: University of California Press, 1925.

Bushnell, Amy Turner. *The King's Coffer: Proprietors of the Spanish Florida Treasury, 1565–1702*. Gainesville, Fla.: University Press of Florida, 1981.

Chatelain, Verne Elmo. *The Defenses of Spanish Florida, 1565–1763*. Publication 511. Washington, D.C.: Carnegie Institute, 1941.

Cline, Howard F. *Notes on Colonial Indians and Communities in Florida, 1700–1821*. Vol. 1 of *Florida Indians*. 3 vols. Garland American Indian Ethnohistory Series. New York: Garland, 1974.

Coe, Charles H. *Red Patriots: The Story of the Seminoles*. Gainesville, Fla.: University Press of Florida, 1974.

Coffman, Edward M. *The Old Army: A Portrait of the American Army in Peacetime, 1784–1898*. New York: Oxford University Press, 1986.

Coker, William S., and Thomas D. Watson. *Indian Traders of the Southeastern Spanish Borderlands: Panton, Leslie and Company, and John Forbes and Company, 1783–1847*. Pensacola, Fla.: University of West Florida Press, 1986.

Cole, Donald B. *Martin Van Buren and the American Political System*. Princeton, N.J.: Princeton University Press, 1984.

Corkran, David H. *The Creek Frontier, 1540–1783*. Norman, Okla.: University of Oklahoma Press, 1967.

Covington, James W. *The Seminoles of Florida*. Gainesville, Fla.: University Press of Florida, 1993.

Craton, Michael. *Testing the Chains: Resistance in Slavery in the British West Indies*. Ithaca, N.Y.: Cornell University Press, 1982.

Crawford, Michael H., ed. *Black Caribs: A Case Study in Biocultural Adaptation*. New York: Plenum Press, 1984.

Creel, Margaret Washington. *"A Peculiar People": Slave Religion and Community Culture among the Gullahs*. New York: New York University Press, 1988.

Fairbanks, Charles H. *Ethnohistorical Report on the Florida Indians*. Vol. 3 of *Florida Indians*. 3 vols. Garland American Indian Ethnohistory Series. New York: Garland, 1974.

Fick, Carolyn E. *The Making of Haiti*. Knoxville: University of Tennessee Press, 1990.

Foner, Jack D. *Blacks and the Military in American History*. New York: Praeger, 1974.

Foreman, Grant. *Indian Removal*. Norman, Okla.: University of Oklahoma Press, 1932.

———. *Advancing the Frontier, 1830–1860*. Norman, Okla.: University of Oklahoma Press, 1933.

———. *The Five Civilized Tribes*. Norman, Okla.: University of Oklahoma Press, 1934.

———. *The Last Trek of the Indians*. Chicago: University of Chicago Press, 1946.

Gatscket, Albert S. *A Migration Legend of the Creek Indians.* 1884. Reprint, New York: AMS Press, 1969.

Genovese, Eugene D. *Roll, Jordan, Roll: The World the Slaves Made.* New York: Pantheon Books, 1974.

Gibson, Arrell M. *The Chickasaws.* Norman, Okla.: University of Oklahoma Press, 1971.

Gonzalez, Nancie L. Solien. *Sojourners of the Caribbean: Ethnogenesis and Ethnohistory of the Garifuna.* Urbana, Ill.: University of Illinois Press, 1988.

Green, Michael D. *The Politics of Indian Removal: Creek Government and Society in Crisis.* Lincoln, Nebr.: University of Nebraska Press, 1982.

Greene, Robert E. *Black Defenders of America, 1775–1973.* Chicago: Johnson Publishing Co., 1974.

Halatsz, Nicholas. *The Rattling Chains: Slave Unrest and Revolt in the Antebellum South.* New York: McKay, Van Rees, 1966.

Herskovits, Melville Jean. *The Myth of the Negro Past.* New York and London: Harper and Bros., 1941.

Joyner, Charles. *Down by the Riverside: A South Carolina Slave Community.* Urbana, Ill.: University of Illinois Press, 1984.

Katz, William Loren. *Black Indians: A Hidden Heritage.* New York: Atheneum, 1986.

———. *The Black West.* 3d ed., rev. and exp. Seattle: Open Hand, 1987.

Landers, Jane. "African Presence in Early Spanish Colonization of the Caribbean and the Southeastern Borderlands." In *Columbian Consequences.* Vol. 2. Ed. David Hurst Thomas. Washington, D.C.: Smithsonian Institution Press, 1989.

Laumer, Frank. *Massacre!* Gainesville, Fla.: University Press of Florida, 1968.

Leckie, William H. *The Buffalo Soldiers: A Narrative of the Negro Cavalry in the West.* Norman, Okla.: University of Oklahoma Press, 1967.

LaFeber, Walter. "Jefferson and an American Foreign Policy." In *Jeffersonian Legacies.* Ed. Peter Onuf. Charlottesville, Va.: University Press of Virginia, 1993.

Littlefield, Daniel C. *Rice and Slaves: Ethnicity and the Slave Trade in Colonial South Carolina.* Baton Rouge, La.: Louisiana State University Press, 1981.

Littlefield, Daniel F. Jr. *Africans and Seminoles: From Removal to Emancipation.* Westport, Conn.: Greenwood Press, 1977.

———. *The Cherokee Freedmen: From Emancipation to American Citizenship.* Westport, Conn.: Greenwood Press, 1978.

———. *Africans and Creeks: From the Colonial Period to the Civil War.* Westport, Conn.: Greenwood Press, 1979.

———. *The Chickasaw Freedmen: A People without a Country.* Westport, Conn.: Greenwood Press, 1980.

Lynch, Dennis Tilden. *An Epoch and a Man.* New York: Horace Liveright, 1929.

Mahon, John K. *History of the Second Seminole War, 1835–1842.* Gainesville, Fla.: University Press of Florida, 1967.

McReynolds, Edwin C. *The Seminoles.* Norman, Okla.: University of Oklahoma Press, 1957.

Meinig, D. W. *The Shaping of America.* Vol. 2. New Haven, Conn.: Yale University Press, 1993.

Mowat, Charles Loch. *East Florida as a British Province, 1763–1784.* Gainesville, Fla.: University Press of Florida, 1964.

Mulroy, Kevin. *Freedom on the Border.* Lubbock, Tex.: Texas Tech University Press, 1993.

Murphy, E. Jefferson. *History of African Civilization.* New York: Crowell, 1972.

Owsley, Frank L. Jr. *The Struggle for the Gulf Borderlands: The Creek War and the Battle of New Orleans.* Gainesville, Fla.: University Press of Florida, 1981.

Parrish, John O. *Battling the Seminoles.* Lakeland, Fla.: Southern Printing, 1930.

Parry, J. H., and P. M. Sherlock. *A Short History of the West Indies.* 2d ed. London: Macmillan Co., 1963.

Parton, James. *Life of Andrew Jackson.* 3 vols. New York: Mason, 1860.

Patrick, Rembert W. *Florida Fiasco: Rampant Rebels on the Georgia-Florida Border, 1810–1815.* Athens, Ga.: University of Georgia Press, 1954.

Peters, Virginia B. *The Florida Wars.* Hamden, Conn.: Archon Books, 1979.

Porter, Kenneth W. *The Negro on the American Frontier.* New York: Arno Press and the New York Times, 1971.

Potter, Woodburne. *The War in Florida, Being an Exposition of Its Causes and an Accurate History of the Campaigns of Generals Clinch, Gaines, and Scott.* Baltimore: Lewis and Coleman, 1936.

Price, Richard, ed. *Maroon Societies: Rebel Slave Communities in the Americas.* Baltimore: Johns Hopkins University Press, 1979.

Priestley, Herbert Ingram. *A History of American Life.* New York: Macmillan Co., 1929.

Quarles, Benjamin. *The Negro in the American Revolution.* New York and London: W. W. Norton and Co.: 1961.

Ressen, Edward. *Jacksonian America.* Rev. ed. Urbana, Ill.: University of Illinois Press, 1985.

Robinson, Carey. *The Fighting Maroons of Jamaica.* Great Britain: William Collins and Sangster, 1869.

Schwarz, Catherine, ed. *Chambers Concise Dictionary.* Edinburgh: W and R Chambers Ltd., 1988.

Shepherd, Edward M. *American Statesman.* Boston and New York: Houghton, Mifflin and Co., 1899.

Silver, James W. *Edmund Pendleton Gaines, Frontier General.* Baton Rouge, La.: Louisiana State University Press, 1949.

Sirmans, Eugene M. *Colonial South Carolina: A Political History, 1663–1763.* Chapel Hill, N.C.: University of North Carolina Press, 1966.

Smith, Joseph B. *The Plot to Steal Florida.* New York: Harbor House, 1983.

Stewart, James Brewer. *Joshua R. Giddings and the Tactics of Radical Politics.* Cleveland, Ohio: Case Western Reserve University Press, 1970.

Sturtevant, William C. "Creek into Seminole." In *North American Indians in Historical Perspective.* Eds. Eleanor B. Leacock and Nancy O. Lurie. New York: Random House, 1971.

Tanner, Helen Hornbeck. *Zéspedes in East Florida, 1784–1790.* Coral Gables, Fla.: University of Miami Press, 1963.

Tebeau, Charlton W. *Man in the Everglades.* Coral Gables, Fla.: University of Miami Press, 1969.

———. *A History of Florida.* Coral Gables, Fla.: University of Miami Press, 1971.

TePaske, John J. *The Governorship of Spanish Florida, 1700–1763.* Durham, N.C.: Duke University Press, 1964.

Thomson, George Malcolm. *Sir Francis Drake.* New York: William Morrow and Co., 1972.

Tyler, Lyon Gardiner. *The American Nation: A History.* Vol. 4, *England in America, 1580–1652.* New York: Harper Brothers, 1904.

Velazquez de la Cadena, Mariano. *New Revised Velazquez Spanish and English Dictionary.* Chicago: Follett Publishing Co., 1974.

Wardell, Morris L. *A Political History of the Cherokee Nation, 1838–1907.* Norman, Okla.: University of Oklahoma Press, 1938.

Webster's Third New International Dictionary. Springfield, Mass.: G. and C. Merriam Co., 1961.

Weir, Robert. *Colonial South Carolina.* Milwood, N.Y.: Kraus Thomson Ltd., 1983.

Wright, Irene A. "The Spanish Resistance to the English Occupation of Jamaica, 1655–1660." In *Transactions of the Royal Historical Society.* Series 4, vol. 13. London: Butler and Tanner Ltd., 1930.

Government Documents

American State Papers: 1, Foreign Relations. Vol. 4.

———: *2, Indian Affairs.* Vols. 1 and 2.

———: *5, Military Affairs.* Vols. 1–7.

Annals of the Congress of the United States, 1789–1824. 42 vols. Washington, D.C., 1834–56.

Biographical Directory of the United States Congress. Washington, D.C.: U.S. Government Printing Office, 1989.

Charles II. *Royal Edict of 1693.* 7 November 1693. John B. Stetson Collection, P. K. Yonge Library of Florida History. Gainesville, Fla.: University of Florida, SD58-1-26.

Coleman, Kenneth, ed. *Trustees Letter Book.* Vol. 31. *The Colonial Records of Georgia, 1745–1752.* Athens, Ga.: University of Georgia Press, 1986.

Coleman, Kenneth, and Milton Ready, eds. "The Original Papers of Governor John Reynolds, 1754–1756." Vol. 28, part 2. In *The Colonial Records of Georgia, 1757–1763.* Athens, Ga.: University of Georgia Press, 1979.

———. "The Original Papers of Governor Reynolds, Ellis, Wright, and Others." Vol. 27. In *The Colonial Records of Georgia, 1757–1763.* Athens, Ga.: University of Georgia Press, 1979.

Congressional Globe. 46 vols. Washington, D.C., 1834–73.

Fitzpatrick, John C., ed. *Journals of the Continental Congress, 1774–1789.* 34 vols. Washington, D.C.: U.S. Government Printing Office, 1904–37.

Kappler, Charles, ed. *Indian Affairs, Laws, and Treaties.* Vol. 2. Washington, D.C.: U.S. Government Printing Office, 1904.

Miller, David Hunter, ed. *Treaties and Other International Acts of the United States of America.* Vol. 2, 1776–1818. Washington, D.C.: U.S. Government Printing Office, 1931.

———. *Treaties and Other International Acts of the United States of America.* Vol. 3, 1819–1835. Washington, D.C.: U.S. Government Printing Office, 1933.

Nichols, Philip. "Sir Francis Drake Revived." Ed. Sir Francis Drake Baronet. In *Documents Concerning English Voyages to the Spanish Main, 1569–1580.* Vol. 71. Ed. Irene A. Wright, 1628. Reprint, Nendeln, Liechtenstein: Kraus Reprint Ltd., 1932, 254–323.

State Papers and Publick Documents of the United States. Series 1. Vol. 9, 3d ed. Boston: Thomas B. Wait, 1819.

United Kingdom, *Journal of the Commissioners for Trade and Plantations, 1764–1767.* London: Her Majesty's Stationery Office, 1986.

———. Public Record Office. *Calendar of State Papers, Colonial Series, 1574–1660.* Vols. 1, 5. Ed. W. Noel Sainsbury. 1860. Reprint, Vaduz, Liechtenstein: Kraus Reprint Ltd., 1964, 122.

———. Public Record Office. "America and the West Indies, 1681–1685," *Calendar of State Papers, Colonial Series.* 2d. ed. Vols. 10, 11, 13, and 17. Ed. J. W. Fortescue. 1898. Reprint, Nendeln, Liechtenstein: Kraus Reprint Ltd., 1964.

U.S. Congress. House. President Tyler reports to the House on how the war is ended. 27th Cong., 2d sess., *Congressional Information Service,* 29 January 1842, H. Doc. 55: 1–9.

———. Senate. Florida Congressman Joseph White demands that General Scott be relieved of the command in the Second Seminole War. 25th Cong., 2d sess., *Congressional Globe*, 11 January 1836, S. Doc. 231. Fiche 378, 6.

———. General Jesup's report to the Senate after retiring from command. 25th Cong., 2d sess., *Congressional Information Service*, 7 July 1838, S. Doc. 507: 11.

Journal Articles

Landers, Jane. "A Free Town in Spanish Colonial Florida." *American Historical Review* 95 (February 1990): 9–30.

Ott, Eloise. "Fort King: A Brief History." *Florida Historical Quarterly* 46 (July 1967): 29–38.

Otto, John S. "Hillsborough County (1850): A Community in the South Florida Flatwoods." *Florida Historical Quarterly* 62 (October 1983): 180–93.

Owsley, Frank L. Jr. "British and Indian Activities in Spanish West Florida during the War of 1812." *Florida Historical Quarterly* 41 (October 1968): 111–40.

McPherson, James M. "The Fight against the Gag Rule: Joshua Leavitt and Antislavery Insurgency in the Whig Party, 1839–42." *Journal of Negro History* 48 (1963): 177–95.

Porter, Kenneth W. "Notes on Seminole Negroes in the Bahamas." *Florida Historical Quarterly* 24 (July 1945): 56–60.

———. "The Founder of the 'Seminole Nation' Secoffee or Cowkeeper." *Florida Historical Quarterly* 27 (April 1949): 362–84.

———. "Billy Bowlegs (Holata Micco) in the Seminole Wars." Part 1. *Florida Historical Quarterly* 45 (January 1967): 219–42.

Sturtevant, William C. "Notes on Modern Seminole Traditions of Osceola." *Florida Historical Quarterly* 33 (January–April 1955): 206–17.

Wright, Irene A., ed. "Dispatches of Spanish Officials Bearing on the Free Negro Settlement of Gracia Real de Santa Teresa de Mose, Florida." *The Journal of Negro History* 9 (1924): 145–95. Author's translation.

Index